Table of Contents

Introduction		i
Chapter 1	How Do We Define Money	1
Chapter 2	Spending Without Money Moving	7
Chapter 3	Central Banks	21
Chapter 4	Money Income, Wealth Income?	42
Chapter 5	Stock and Flow! OH NO!	50
Chapter 6	Savings	61
Chapter 7	Correcting GDP	63
Chapter 8	Sectoral Balances	85
Chapter 9	MMT Alleges that Increasing Government Debt is Required to have Increasing Private Domestic Wealth	93
Chapter 10	The Function of Treasury Borrowing	111
Chapter 11	Interest Rates on Bonds And IOER	114
Chapter 12	Functional Finance	117

A Critique of Modern Monetary Theory

Based on the concepts introduced in the Book "Enlightened Capitalism: A Keynes Primer"

Daniel Bright M.D.

outskirts
press

A Critique of Modern Monetary Theory
Based on the concepts introduced in the Book "Enlightened Capitalism: A Keynes Primer"
All Rights Reserved.
Copyright © 2023 Daniel Bright M.D.
v10.0

The opinions expressed in this manuscript are solely the opinions of the author and do not represent the opinions or thoughts of the publisher. The author has represented and warranted full ownership and/or legal right to publish all the materials in this book.

This book may not be reproduced, transmitted, or stored in whole or in part by any means, including graphic, electronic, or mechanical without the express written consent of the publisher except in the case of brief quotations embodied in critical articles and reviews.

Outskirts Press, Inc.
http://www.outskirtspress.com

ISBN: 978-1-9772-5829-8

Library of Congress Control Number: 2022919798

Cover Photo © 2023 www.gettyimages.com. All rights reserved - used with permission.

Outskirts Press and the "OP" logo are trademarks belonging to Outskirts Press, Inc.

PRINTED IN THE UNITED STATES OF AMERICA

Use Your QR App
To Learn More Today

Introduction

This book is intended as an analysis of some of the most central concepts upon which Modern Monetary Theory (MMT) is based. The analysis will be based on my understanding of macroeconomics which I have introduced in the book "Enlightened Capitalism: A Keynes Primer", 2nd Edition. I will be attempting to fit the MMT model into my model, and not the other way around. So, this book is as much an introduction to, and expansion of, my work as it is a study of the basic tenets of MMT. Understanding this critique will require one to be familiar with the concepts presented in the above mentioned book. If you decide to take on the task of mastering the material in this volume I suggest keeping "Enlightened Capitalism: A Keynes Primer", 2nd Edition available for easy reference.

CHAPTER 1
How Do We Define Money

Since this is a book discussing Modern Monetary Theory (MMT), I thought it would be good to spend some time trying to understand money and its function.

WHAT IS MONEY?

What types of currencies do we have and what is the money supply?

A currency is one of those commodities that has been established in the economy as being used as money. To be a currency, that item must be something that holds its value, is convenient to use and does not involve significant costs for its storage or use in spending. Just to mention, I will generally be using the words currency and money interchangeably.

No economy has now or ever had its money supply consist completely of one type or denomination of currency.

In fact, anything that is ever traded might be considered a currency, with the interpretation of what the cutoff should be for what is meant by "holding its value", "significant cost of storage", and

How Do We Define Money

being considered "easily tradable" all being things that are highly subjective.

If the money supply were to include certain items used in trade then the spending created with a particular one of those items would be defined as the total value of the entire supply of that item, multiplied by the average number of times each unit of that "money" (the item) was exchanged in trade, during that time period.

So let us say that we determined that we should count as money "n" different things. And the total value of the entire supply of the jth item is Mj. And let us define Vj as the average number of times each unit of that "currency" is used for spending during a given time period, (Vj is the Velocity of spending of Mj). Then the contribution of that particular "currency" to total spending is Mj times Vj (Mj*Vj). And if we include all the spending of any item we have decided to include as a currency, in this particular economy, for the given time period, total spending would equal:

$M_1 * V_1$ plus

$M_2 * V_2$ plus

$M_3 * V_3$ plus

$M_4 * V_4$ plus

$M_5 * V_5$ plus

$M_6 * V_6$ plus

.

.

.

How Do We Define Money

$M_{(n-2)} * V_{(n-2)}$ plus

$M_{(n-1)} * V_{(n-1)}$ plus

$M_n * V_n$

That is the way to try to add together transactions done with any item used for spending so as to calculate a value for total spending. One would multiply the total value of the entire supply of the particular item we are considering to be money, times the average number of times each unit of that item is used for spending, to get the contribution to spending from transactions done with that item. Then one would add that value to the total. Do that for every item considered being used as currency, add their contribution to the total, and when all the different currencies' spending is accounted for, you have a value for total spending for that economy.

Notice that the spending that occurs for each item is not the total value of the entire supply of that item, but is the total value of all the units of that item *times* the average number of times each unit is used for spending. If we are talking dollars, and we have a total of 100 dollars, and the average number of times each dollar is spent is 10 times, then the dollar contribution to total spending is 1000 dollars, not 100 dollars.

The items we consider to be money could include fiat money, IOUs, or representative money such as gold standard money. We could even decide that certain items commonly used in barter would be better classified as currencies. However, allowing all things that may ever be used for trade to be considered a currency, would make a definition of the money supply so complicated and so constantly changing in total value, that it would lose much of its usefulness in applying the information to macroeconomic analysis, models and policy recommendations

For one thing, if we go back to the definition of a good currency, a lot of items will not qualify because their value is constantly changing and unreliable, such as commodities whose value is always either increasing or decreasing, caused by changing valuation or changes in quantity of the items, either from more being created, (perhaps for use in purposes other than as a currency), or from the items depreciating in value, or being destroyed or depleted. Or the items may count as not favorable for use as currencies because of costs involved in storage or in conducting the actual transactions. All of which would need to be considered in accounting for the effect of a given quantity of spending on the economy. Again, such a thing could get very complicated.

When we are talking about "what is money" we note that over time certain items became looked at as favorable items for use in trade, and use as a currency became an important role for those items. We do not include, in our calculations for total spending, all transactions that occur in an economy, because we do not include every commodity involved in some transactions as being a currency, but items that qualify as a good currency we might include. There could potentially be a significant number of such commodities, and accounting for this could still get very complicated. However, I suggest this is really not such a problem. If, when it comes to what gets counted as a currency, we only include those things that are used for the *vast majority* of spending, and we exclude things that give a much smaller contribution (such as orders of magnitude smaller in most cases), the result is we can greatly decrease the number of items we need to recognize as currencies and are used for our calculations of total spending.

In fact, I suggest that for most economies, spending is dominated by the country's sovereign currency, (i.e., the money created by a given country's Central Bank), so much so, that if we only use the sovereign currency to calculate our total spending, it will give a pretty good accounting of what total spending is occurring and its effect. This is pretty much what Modern Monetary Theory proponents refer to when they are talking about money, specifically "base money". So, I will also make that assumption, that when we are talking about spending, we are defining this as the transfer of ownership of base money, where this base money is the sovereign currency of that country, or some country at least.

It is possible to argue that one can focus on spending of the main sovereign currency even though we recognize that there are other activities going on, contributing to the economy, wealth creation and depletion, which are not explicitly related to the transfer of ownership of that sovereign currency. This might even include transactions that could be counted as spending of a second or third currency but was not included in our model.

Recognizing that we cannot include every item involved in trade as a currency, we must make the cutoff somewhere. For our purposes the cutoff is defined as only including sovereign currency as what we consider to be money, base money that is.

If someone finds it unacceptable to only include the sovereign currency to calculate total spending, and they wanted to include other things as currency, they will need to use the formula shown above where each currency's contribution to spending is calculated by multiplying the total value of the existing supply of that currency times the average velocity of spending of each unit of that currency.

How Do We Define Money

One thing I have a different view on than most, is the description that bank deposits are considered money. I consider bank deposits to be assets, not money, and that all spending involving the currency used in the creation and manipulation of those bank deposits, can be understood as occurring due to the transfer of ownership of base money. I have discussed this in detail in the book "Enlightened Capitalism: A Keynes Primer".

CHAPTER 2
Spending Without Money Moving

This is not a concept that Modern Monetary Theory (MMT) directly addresses but if you do not understand this concept, you cannot understand modern economics in general.

THE CONCEPT OF spending without money moving, presented in chapter 3 of "Enlightened Capitalism: A Keynes Primer", is an important one which appears to be under-appreciated in modern economic theory. One of the most important things that understanding this concept does is to allow us to simplify our models and understand spending and income and the money supply in less complex ways.

It also allows us to properly understand the savings equals investment identity and to properly understand something called "Sectoral Balances". Sectoral Balances is a theoretical concept that is central to Modern Monetary Theory, as taught by its proponents.

As I mentioned in the last chapter, in my book "Enlightened Capitalism: A Keynes Primer" I described how, in my opinion, it was much simpler to describe bank deposits as assets, based on a debt obligation of the bank to the depositor, rather than as money.

Spending Without Money Moving

I described how all the actual spending that occurs in the fractional reserve banking system is done by the transfer of ownership of base money. As such, I then describe how we should understand the fractional reserve banking system as causing an increase in the velocity of spending of that base money, rather than causing an increase in the money supply.

Also in that book, I noted that for my model to accurately describe reality, one must use a modified definition of base money, specifically that money owned by the Treasury MUST be included in what we call the base money supply. I mention money owned by the Treasury because standard economics specifically excludes Treasury owned money from their definition of the base money supply.

I have a much more exact definition of the [sovereign currency fiat] base money supply. I define the base money supply as including any money owned by entities other than the Central Bank, and which is therefore available to be used for spending by those entities. But if any of that money becomes owned by the Central Bank then it is no longer in the money supply.

Now I could be missing something that gets excluded from money supply in the standard definition, but so far as I know it is only the Treasury that is specifically excluded from the definition of the base money supply as normally taught. If I have missed something, and there are other places that money which, according to my more exact definition, should not have been excluded from the base money supply but was, then, to avoid confusion, one can just revert to using the more exact definition of the fiat base money supply I just described, that is, money is in the money supply when it is owned by entities other than the Central Bank. I should clarify that domestic sovereign currency owned by a foreign country's Central Bank should be considered to be in the domestic country's base money supply. At any rate, please note that

Spending Without Money Moving

my definition of the base money supply is modified from how it is usually taught.

Money spending without moving is central to understanding these concepts. Money spending without money moving can occur because the definition of spending is the transfer of ownership of money, which does not require the money to change its physical location. This type of spending depends heavily on accurate and honest record keeping. And this is what I wanted to look at a little closer in this section.

The fractional reserve banking system is a somewhat complex structure that can be interpreted and explained as functioning so that all spending is done by the transfer of ownership of **base** money. But it is a system where the availability of money for spending by individuals is heavily dependent on the paying back of loans, which occurs over time. Thus, there are limits to how much of the total deposits existing in the banking system, at any given time, can be withdrawn and used to support all the depositors' desired spending.

"Enlightened Capitalism: A Keynes Primer" explains how depositors do not ever really "own" the money they have in their bank deposits (unless they withdraw it from the bank in physical form, notes or coins), but the depositors can direct the spending of that amount of money. In such a case, records will show transactions that occurred where ownership of the money was transferred from being owned by the buyer's bank to being owned by the seller's bank.

It is simplest to understand this transaction if we think of how this transaction would work if the spending involved the physical exchange of physical money. For that to happen, the entity who

Spending Without Money Moving

wants to spend some of his deposit money would liquidate part of his bank deposit, meaning he would request the bank to give him cash in lieu of part of the bank deposit. The buyer would then physically hand the cash to the seller of the item being purchased. This seller would then give that cash to his own bank in exchange for a bank deposit of that amount. In that process the ownership and physical possession of the money would be transferred from the buyer's bank, to the buyer, to the seller, to the seller's bank. That would mean that as the cash moved it would have its ownership and physical possession change at least 3 times.

Because of the phenomenon of money being spent without physically moving, most transactions do not need to occur with physical money being exchanged. The description of a transaction occurring with physical money changing hands, is in essence, what is occurring in all transactions, but for spending done without money moving, we do not "see" the part where the money is temporarily owned by the buyer and then the seller of the item being purchased. Instead, even though the item purchased may physically change hands, (depending on what is bought), physical possession of the money being spent does not . All we see is the buyer's bank owning the money and a debt obligation to the buyer, and then, after the transaction, ownership of the money has transferred to the seller's bank which then would owe a debt obligation (bank deposit) of the amount of the sale to the seller. So, after the transaction is finalized, the records will show which bank owns the cash spent (and a debt to its depositor) and whose bank deposit ends up larger and whose ends up smaller.

If the buyer and seller have the same bank, the ownership of the money stays with that bank, but that bank's records reflect that money is being owed by the bank to the seller and not the buyer anymore. At any rate, the ownership of the money has changed from one bank to another or at least from one account of the same bank to another. Either way we can look at this as the transfer of ownership of money, which is the definition of spending. In this case, it is spending which has occurred without the physical transfer of money.

The type of money i am talking about in most of the "spending without money moving" scenarios is money stored at the Central Bank. Most of which is virtual money, declared as existing by the Central Bank and kept track of on a ledger. This is money I describe as "Stored at the Central Bank but owned the Commercial Banks". When ownership of money changes, instead of money physically moving, the Central Bank just adjusts its records to reflect which entity, that is, which Commercial Bank, has come to **own** that money.

Should We Call Bank Deposits Money?

One could call the bank deposits themselves "money" and imply that the spending that occurred, occurred by the spending of that "bank deposit money". If that were the case, you could state that bank deposits are IOU's that have become money and are always causing the money supply to increase and decrease as bank deposits are created or paid off.

In fact, that is how the money supply is normally described. This is where you get the idea of all these different money supplies, M_B, M_0, M_1, M_2, etc., where the money supplies are always changing. Most of the M's represent a mixture of base money and bank deposits, (or if not actually bank deposits they are loan obligations of some sort). Now, calling bank deposits money may have its use but doing so obscures what is happening with base money, and it obscures the effects of interventions done by the Central Bank when they increase or decrease the base money supply.

Spending Without Money Moving

These two factors just mentioned: thinking of bank deposits as money and not including money owned by the Treasury as being in the money supply, are two factors that, in my view, make it very difficult to get a handle on what the money supply is.

As a result of categorizing bank deposits as money, it is common in modern macroeconomic teaching to promote the idea that Commercial Banks create most of our money "out of thin air". This idea leads people to believe that there is no definable money supply, or to begin to lose faith in the future buying power of their money. In turn, this leads to the development of all sorts of conspiracy theories about the banking system. A clear, simple understanding of the definition of the base money supply is, in my view, essential to developing a basic and correct understanding of macroeconomic theory. In my model, I try to develop an understanding of money that allows a solid handle on what we are counting as money, and the size of the money supply.

If one thinks of bank deposits as money, one could look at it as an IOU or perhaps as a representative money whose value is based on how much of it is backed by Commercial Bank reserves (all of which is base money) and how much by debt. But since there is an underlying mechanism, money spending without money moving, that allows us to understand that the money whose ownership is being changed, is the base money (my definition, which includes money owned by the Treasury), then I suggest it is best to look at bank deposits as assets and not as money.

But are there things one might consider as representative money when its value comes solely from a debt obligation? Describing an asset this way would require that the owner of that asset be able to cash it in for base money. This makes it a purely financial asset (as defined in "Enlightened Capitalism"),

Spending Without Money Moving

as the holder is owed a debt of base money upon which the assets value rests.

Can a purely financial asset be considered to be a currency? I find that for the most part it is best if we only consider it an asset, not money. I believe that in such a case, it makes economics easier to get a handle on, if at every opportunity we consider spending to be the transfer of ownership of base money. And that the spending of that base money occurs by the method previously described, where we have at least a 3 step transaction. And when we have money being spent without money moving, the part where buyer and seller temporarily own the money is happening "behind the scenes". For assets handled this way, the asset owner can direct the spending of an amount equal to some or all of the value of their asset, but the asset would still not be considered money. In such transactions, the ownership of the money used for the purchase then goes from the entity owing a debt obligation to the buyer for the original asset to the entity owing the debt obligation to the seller for the seller's newly produced or increased asset.

Perhaps there are situations where such IOU's function as a currency, with spending not involving the cashing in of some sovereign currency. This is more likely to occur in a country where the sovereign currency is unstable and unreliable. The value of such IOUs could possibly be attached to some other country's sovereign currency. If such a manipulation caused a significant amount of increase in spending, then one might consider looking at those IOUs as a currency. However, even here, one could consider the spending of the IOUs to really occur by the transfer of ownership of the base money which backs the value of those IOUs. In such a case the spending may involve accounts at the Commercial or Central Banks of the country whose currency gives the IOU value. Or this could possibly be a situation where the record keeping determining who owns the base money in question, is done by entities outside the banking system, that is, not by

Spending Without Money Moving

any banks, Commercial or Central. An example of a representative money backed, ultimately, by fiat money, that worked for a time as a currency would be the use of cell phone calling minutes as a currency mentioned in the book, "Enlightened Capitalism: A Keynes Primer".

In modern times, the currency functioning as the base money is almost always fiat money. In the past, gold standard money has certainly operated as money, and could perhaps still be considered as such, except that gold and any certificates that represent ownership of gold no longer function as a good currency and can only really be looked at as a commodity. One thing that keeps it from functioning as a good currency is the constant and often dramatic swings in its valuation.

Checks, as in checking accounts, can be looked at as money if it were used in such a way that the actual paper check became transferred from person to person, but the paper check really just represents a one-time spending of base money, and so is not money.

Credit cards are clearly, like checks, just records of a one-time transfer of ownership of base money, from the bank of the purchaser to the bank of the seller. Though until the credit card balance from that transaction is paid off, it represents the purchase of a loan from the bank issuing the credit card. The interest paid is spending of fiat money to pay for all the services provided to the credit card holder, and the convenience of having the credit card to use. The payment of interest and fees is direct spending, a concept I describe in "Enlightened Capitalism: A Keynes Primer".

Representative money got its start as receipts for items of wealth that could be obtained by presenting the receipt to the owner of that item. One could say it is possible to have representative money operating in the current economy, but, if we do, it is not a significant contributor to overall spending. If the owner of an item needs money, it does not create an IOU based on the

Spending Without Money Moving

presumed cash value of that item and use it as money. Instead, they take out a loan where the item of value may be used as collateral. The loan paperwork is proof of the debt the loan creates, but that paperwork does not circulate being used as a currency for spending. It is base money that circulates being used as currency for the spending. For me, it is always better to understand transactions by how, underneath it all, the spending occurring is the transfer of ownership of base money.

At any rate, I think it is a reasonably accurate approximation to look at the money supply as the amount of base money, (with the caveat that we are including money owned by the Treasury in the definition of base money). Essential to understanding all this is realizing that much of the spending of this base money is spending done without the physical transfer of money. Realizing this goes a long way in allowing us to understand our modern economy.

Do Banks Lend Out Their Reserves?

Some MMT proponents will say that "Banks don't loan out their reserves". Since reserves is another word for "the amount of cash banks own", they are alleging that banks don't loan the cash they own, they just "create money out of thin air" by creating a bank deposit for a borrower.

This is exactly the type of "money spending" that can be understood as spending occurring without the money physically moving. The fact is, the issuing of a loan is the spending of money. It is the bank spending to purchase a debt obligation in the amount of the loan. As a result, ownership of the money changes hands.

Spending Without Money Moving

This is the spending of money, and it cannot occur without... uh.... money.

When the bank approves the loan and the person signs the promissory note, at that point the bank is owed a debt obligation, that is, the bank owns a purely financial asset whose value is based on the amount of the loan.

In return the borrower is given a bank deposit in the same amount from the same bank, which is a debt obligation of the bank to that borrower. That bank deposit is not cash but is a another purely financial asset. At this point both the borrower and the lending bank have gained an asset and a debt obligation.

The borrower controls the spending of an amount of money equal to the size of the bank deposit the lending bank created for them. That money will get used for spending, but at this point it is still owned by the lending bank. When it gets spent, ownership of the money changes, from the bank of the borrower, who is directing the spending, to the bank of the seller of whatever the borrower wanted to purchase. The seller, in return, gets a larger bank deposit.

If the borrower wants to direct the spending of the entirety of the money borrowed, such as when they are buying a house, it starts with the lending bank owning the cash and the borrower owning the asset called a bank deposit. The bank deposit, created at the time of the loan, has value because the lending bank owns the amount of cash the borrower would get if it liquidated the full amount of the bank deposit. The lending bank either has the cash, or can quickly get it, which is saying the bank is lending its reserves. If it were paper money or coins that were physically changing hands everyone would know what is going on and have no doubt that the Commercial Bank is "loaning out its money".

However, in this case, the money, the spending of which the loan recipient now controls, is only UNDERSTOOD to be going to the

Spending Without Money Moving

borrower who gives it to the seller of the house, who puts it in his bank. What happens, in reality, is the original lender marks its records, to state that the money is no longer owed to the original borrower, but is now owned by the bank of the seller of the house. The seller's bank, in return, owes a debt obligation called a bank deposit, in the amount of the sale of the house, to the seller. So, the ownership of the money has transferred to the seller's bank. The borrower no longer has the bank deposit, but still owes a debt obligation to the original lending bank and of course, now owns the house.

The selling has not caused any physical movement of the cash, the spending has all occurred by being documented in the records of the banks involved in the transaction. But the transaction **did** involve transfer of ownership of the money that was part of the lending bank's reserves. It did, therefore, involve the spending of the lending bank's money, its reserves. It is just that it was "spending without money moving", spending that occurred solely with the adjustment of records.

In order for this to work, the bank receiving the money, the bank of the house seller, has to trust that the original bank, the bank that loaned to the borrower, is good for the money. Being good for the money is equivalent to saying the bank loaned out its money, its reserves, i.e., it has the money, or can certainly easily get it. Eventually banks must "settle accounts" and when the time comes, the lending bank better have the money, or at least prove that is owns that amount of money so that ownership of that amount of money can be reflected as going to the bank of the house seller.

Settling accounts means adjusting records so that, in the simplest possible way, everybody knows how much money each bank owns. Which to me would mean keeping the type of records they would need to be providing to the Central Bank on a regular basis.

In the meantime, while waiting to settle accounts, other transactions might take place where the records show the 1st bank controlling money owned by the 2nd bank and others where the 2nd bank is controlling money owned by the 1st bank, and there might be multiple other banks involved as well. When they settle accounts, all the banks use the net of what has changed in the ownership of money to determine how much money the records should show they each own.

Settling accounts does involve reporting to the Central Bank as well, including reporting the net of what has happened to the amount of money owned by each Commercial Bank, that is, what their total reserves are, at the end of a given time period.

Money spending without money moving is based on record keeping. But it is real spending of real money. It is not the magical creation of money "out of thin air". If it was magical then we all ought to be able to issue loans. The reason banks can lend is because when the actual cash needs to be spent, i.e., when ownership of the cash needs to change, they own that cash, meaning they are "good for it". Even if being good for it means the Commercial Bank has to get a loan from the Central Bank at the last minute to increase its reserves enough to make good on a loan the bank dispensed. They are still good for it, and they are still lending their cash, that is, they are lending the base money they own. Commercial Banks can get loans directly from the Central Banks under certain circumstances, and this is a situation where new money is created "out of thin air", but by the Central Bank, not the Commercial Bank.

Bretton Woods

Historically our monetary system was defined by and subject to a set of rules known as the Bretton Woods system, now defunct. This was basically an attempt at having a worldwide gold standard system, and an attempt at a single currency economy. Why do I say single currency economy? Because the exchange rate for all the different currencies needed to be maintained as constant within a small range so it was the same as if we had one currency. Currencies were pegged to the value of the US dollar and the value of the dollar was pegged to gold.

This system from the beginning was rigged in favor of certain countries' economies and did not allow flexible currency policies that poorer countries might be able to use to improve their competitiveness in trade. Many nations found themselves in debt as well, with debt affecting their ability to be competitive. Eventually, due to several reasons, the Bretton Woods system collapsed. Around 1971 the United States abandoned that system, and the rest of the world quickly followed suit. Since then, the US and other countries have operated under the modern fiat money banking systems we currently have.

As an example of how the Bretton Woods system became problematic, let us say a country was able to sell the US their exports. The US would have to exchange dollars, for example, for francs, if the trade was with France. That would cause the dollar to depreciate compared to the franc. But that was not allowed. So even though France increased their income by efficiently producing desirable products, they would then have to use francs to exchange for dollars increasing the value of the dollar compared to the franc and reducing the value of the franc to the allowed exchange rate level. That would cause any assets denominated in francs to lose value.

Now if France was importing US goods, they would have to exchange francs to get dollars to buy those goods, driving down the value of the franc. This was not allowed and the only way the to appreciate the value of the franc and get its value back up is for France to use its "dollar reserves" to purchase back francs. They could only do so until their dollar reserves ran out at which point, they would need to borrow to have more dollars. This would increase the debt of the French.

Now, France, or any other country could also have its own gold. This would be desirable because gold could be exchanged for dollars, meaning owning gold was as good as having more dollar reserves, in terms of being able to keep their currency's exchange rate stable. Countries figured this out and tried to purchase and own gold, and this began to deplete some of the US gold reserves, threatening the ability of the US to provide enough gold or dollars backed by gold. That was just one of the problems. The point is, the Bretton Woods system began to unravel, and was no longer viable.

Since the system favored rich countries and was a major burden to debtor nations, the economist John Maynard Keynes, wanted the Bretton Woods system to be set up so that if debt became excessive for debtor nations, such that as a result it was not possible for that country's economy to recover, part of the debt could be forgiven by the richer countries. The idea was that there would be a world bank that would monitor these things and negotiate and facilitate the transactions.

At the time of the Bretton Woods conference, at the end of WWII, the United States was the major world creditor and much of Europe, for example, was heavily indebted to the US. Because of this the US held the upper hand in most negotiations and wanted nothing to do with Keynes' debt forgiveness programs. Ultimately, I believe, this decision by the US contributed to the Bretton Woods collapse. Some similar issues regarding certain countries debt were causing trouble in the Euro Zone in recent times.

CHAPTER 3
CENTRAL BANKS

In any country, especially those that have their own Central Bank, there tends to be a dominant currency. Now-a-days the dominant currency is usually what is called fiat currency. And that dominant fiat currency is the currency whose supply is controlled by the Central Bank.

THE TERM "GOVERNMENT", when it comes to macroeconomics is probably not the best label to apply. This is because there are really two parts people refer to when talking about the government and how it is involved in our economy.

One part is what is called the Central Bank. Other than some administrative tasks and oversight functions, its main function is to control the money supply. The Central Bank was purposefully created with limited functions but also with a large degree of independence from elected officials and politicians. The Central Bank increases the base money supply by "creating money out of thin air", [i.e., declaring it as existing in the case of virtual money, or ordering its production in the case of physical money], and uses that money to buy stuff. The Central Bank reduces the money supply by selling stuff. However, and this is important, the Central Bank has severe restrictions on what it can buy and sell. Mostly it buys and sells Treasury bonds. These Treasury Bonds are not purchased directly from the Treasury but from people or entities who already own them. Since the time of the financial crisis in 2008 the Central Bank began to buy large quantities of something called Mortgage Backed Securities (MBS). At any rate, as soon as the Central Bank purchases the Treasury Bond or the MBS, that money becomes part of the base money supply. The Central Bank then "owns" those assets called Treasury bonds and MBS and those assets are then considered to be "on the Central Banks balance sheet". To reduce the money supply, the Central Bank would sell some of the assets on its balance sheet, at which point the money returns to the Central Bank and is no longer in the base money supply.

Since assets on a balance sheet are constantly being paid off (the Central Bank is selling back part of the debt obligation it is owed), then money is always leaving the private sector and becoming owned by the Central Bank, and therefore becomes "out of the money supply", but generally the Central Bank buys more assets, like MBS and Treasury bonds, whose value is based on debt obligations, if it wants to keep the balance sheet stable. I just wanted to mention that allowing debt to be paid off and not replacing it is another way to reduce the money supply.

The other part of the government we refer to here, is any of the federal, state, and local institutions that have anything to do with government spending, taxing, and borrowing. The most important of these institutions is the Treasury. The spending, taxing, and borrowing by these institutions is generally controlled by elected officials and politicians .

Commercial Bank reserves, i.e., money owned by the Commercial Banks or other depository institutions, are in large part stored at the Central Bank. Notice I said stored at the Central Bank, not owned by the Central Bank. Money that becomes owned by the Central Bank goes out of the base money supply and can

Central Banks

be considered as no longer existing. Money "stored at the Central Bank but owned by the Commercial Banks" continues to exist. That money can be physical money, but more likely is virtual money whose existence is recorded on a ledger at the Central Bank, having been declared as existing by the Central Bank at some point in time. Individuals can own money they physically possess, but when those individuals deposit their money in a Commercial Bank, or if money gets transferred from another bank to their account that deposit money becomes owned by that Commercial Bank, while the depositor owns an asset called a bank deposit, which is a debt the Commercial Bank owes to the depositor. Most of that money deposited, that has become owned by the Commercial Banks, is money "stored at the Central Bank but owned by the Commercial Banks". Note that the depositors themselves *cannot* have money "owned by the depositor and stored at the Central Bank". Only certain institutions can have their reserves "stored at the Central Bank", including Commercial Banks, and the Treasury.

There are a couple other institutions, that can have money "owned by them and stored at the Central Bank" called Government Sponsored Enterprises (GSEs). They are commonly referred to as Fannie Mae, and Freddie Mac. These are considered private institutions but were started with support of the government to help increase "liquidity" in the loan market, and facilitate mortgage lending for people who might not otherwise be able to obtain mortgage loans. Performing a similar function is the Government National Mortgage Association often referred to as Ginnie Mae, a U.S. government agency.

These agencies would buy out loans from Commercial Banks, giving those banks money to issue more loans. They would then package the various loans they bought out, into "securities" that they would sell to investors. To my understanding these securities are in the same category as, and include, the previously mentioned Mortgage Backed Securities (MBS), securities whose value is based on the value of the mortgage loans packaged into any particular security. The value of and risk from these securities can vary depending on the financial health of the borrowers of those loans. Apparently the vast majority of these MBS are issued by the three agencies mentioned above.

In 2008, during the financial crisis, many people were defaulting on mortgage loans, and this caused many of these MBS to lose value causing a risk of default across the economy and for many investors. One of the remedies tried to deal with the crisis was to have the Central Bank buy out MBS in large quantities. This stopped many of the investors in those securities from losing as much money and helped stabilize the economy. Why did they choose to help bail out the investors this way?... instead of the alternative?... (which would be, helping the defaulting homeowners directly, so they didn't have to default). I don't know, but that is what happened. Actually, to be fair, over time programs designed help homeowners avoid foreclosure were developed, but it was too little, too late for many homeowners. To my understanding the purchases of MBS were supposed to be a temporary thing, but more than a decade later the balance sheet of the Federal Reserve Bank, America's Central Bank, contains MBS totaling over 2 Trillion dollars.

At any rate, one reason I brought up these agencies, Ginnie Mae, Freddie Mac, and Fannie Mae, is because they too can have their money "owned by them but stored at the Central Bank", meaning like the Commercial Banks they can have accounts at the Central Bank where money they own is "stored". Since money owned by Fannie, Freddie, and Ginny counts as part of the money supply that is not owned by the Treasury, then when calculating the total size of the money supply it is relevant to remember that, other than physical money owned by entities outside the banking system, most of money supply consists of Commercial Bank reserves, Treasury reserves, and reserves of Fannie, Freddie, and Ginny.

But only the Commercial Banks get paid interest on their reserves, most importantly interest on excess reserves (discussed later). Fannie, Freddie, and Ginny, can have reserves, including reserves "held at the Central Bank but owned by Fannie, Freddie, or Ginny" but unlike Commercial Banks they do NOT get paid interest on those reserves. I suspect this would mean there is an incentive for Fannie, Freddie, and Ginny to convert the money in their reserves to interest paying assets, by lending that money to Commercial Banks, who can pay them an interest rate less than the interest paid on Commercial Bank reserves and both the banks and Fannie, Freddie, and Ginny would make a bigger profit than if Fannie, Freddie, and Ginny just held onto their reserves. However, it is my understanding that Fannie, Freddie, and Ginny are required to keep minimum balances of their reserves, and so are limited in their ability to do that. From a practical standpoint, what this means, (Fannie, Freddie, and Ginny needing to hold onto their reserves as minimum balances), is that when money is switching back and forth between Treasury reserves and private reserves it will be switching between Treasury reserves and Commercial Bank reserves. An exception would be during times when the Central Bank is purchasing large quantities of MBS, flooding those agencies with cash. In that situation they could then convert much of that cash into assets that give them a return, needing to only keep that minimum required balance held as reserves.

The depositors and borrowers who support the private domestic banking system are generally private entities. But it is my understanding that state and local institutions use the regular banking system, so they would be like the private domestic depositors, such that when they deposit money in depository institutions, those institutions own the money and the state and local governments own the asset whose value is based on the depository institution's debt to them.

The Treasury is different than state and local government in that, like Commercial Banks, the Treasury can directly "own" money and have its own reserves "stored at the Central Bank", i.e., "stored at the Central Bank but owned by the Treasury". When talking about reserves here we mean all of the money an institution owns, stored at the Central Bank or not. This means that other than physical money, notes and coins, stored outside the depository banking system, and outside the Treasury, the rest of the base money supply is either in Commercial Bank reserves, or in Treasury reserves, with a small amount in reserves of Fannie, Freddie and Ginnie. This will be important when we talk about how the size of the money supply may affect the economy and how MMT advocates look at that issue.

Why is money owned by the Central Bank considered out of the money supply and no longer existing? When money becomes owned by the Central Bank, that money can be burned or destroyed and that will have no effect on Central Bank spending since the Central Bank can create more money any time it wants or needs to. Any money that becomes owned by the Central Bank is completely irrelevant to Central Bank spending, and no longer needs to be accounted for or considered as existing.

The rest of the government, including the Treasury must, on the other hand, obtain money for spending by borrowing or taxing or earning it as income by selling some good or service. The Treasury cannot just create money and use it for spending. MMT implies that the Treasury CAN create money and put it in the money supply. Because, by saying money owned by the Treasury is not in the money supply, if the Treasury spends, the money used goes into the money supply as ownership transfers to the private sector. Still whether money owned by the Treasury is considered in the money supply or not, the Treasury must first acquire that money from some other entity before they can spend it.

Central Banks

Open Market Operations used to be the standard way for the Central Bank to control interest rates. This was done by the adjusting of the size of the money supply to affect the rate of borrowing by one Commercial Bank from another. Commercial Banks need money to lend but they are also (or used to be) required to have a certain amount of money on hand, so there would be money available to customers who want to withdraw their money. This amount is called the required reserve and is usually a percent of the total amount of deposits the Commercial Bank has.

The Central Bank could affect the interest rate Commercial Banks pay to get enough money to meet the reserve requirement and have money to lend. This was accomplished by adjusting the money supply, increasing it or decreasing it . The way this worked is that the more the money supply is increased, the more money is available in Commercial Bank reserves, and thus the cheaper it was for the banks who had a shortage of reserves, to borrow from banks with a surplus of reserves. In such a setting it was easier for the borrowing banks to negotiate a lower rate . On the other hand, the smaller the money supply, the less excess reserves will be available, and the higher the rate borrowing banks will have to pay to get the money to meet their reserve requirements. If banks with reserve shortages found it difficult to borrow from other banks at reasonable rates because excess reserve amounts were too low, they could borrow directly from the Central Bank at the "discount rate" which is set by the Central Bank at a rate higher than the targeted federal funds rate . You will note this is also a way to increase the money supply.

During the Open Market Operations era, a concept that some economists including MMT proponents liked to push is that

Central Banks

Treasury actions can force the Central Bank to create more money or to reduce the money supply. They argue that increased Treasury spending (or reduced taxing or reduced borrowing) increases the private money supply reserves which will cause a reduction in the federal fund rates. This is because money spent by the Treasury usually ends up in Commercial Banks as part of their reserves. Increasing the Commercial Bank reserves would lead to a decrease in the federal funds rate. Since the Central Bank targets the federal funds rate, if the rate goes down the Central Bank would reduce the money supply to increase the interest rates back to target. Similarly, they argue that increased Treasury borrowing, or taxing (or reduced spending) would reduce private reserves and cause an increase in the interest rate above the target rate. This they claim, would force the Central Bank to increase the money supply causing the federal funds rate to be lowered back to the federal funds target. So, they describe an opposite effect where increased Treasury spending would cause the Central Bank to decrease the money supply and reduced Treasury spending would cause the Central Bank to increase the money supply. Thus, some MMT proponents would allege that Treasury actions obligate Central Bank actions, and they are not really independent, because all Central Bank actions and Treasury actions are tied together.

I strongly disagree with that conclusion.

The Treasury only borrows money or taxes to get money it needs to pay for spending. As soon as it gets that money it spends it to pay debt or to pay for all the other things government spending pays for. It does not hold on to that money and build up a supply of unspent money. There is a constant flow of money into and out of the Treasury. If money is to be spent by the Treasury, most of it is obtained from Commercial Bank reserves by taxing or borrowing. If money comes to the Treasury from Commercial Bank reserves as taxing or borrowing, most of it immediately goes right back into Commercial Bank reserves because of the Treasury spending. The amount of money going from the private domestic sector to the Treasury will always be matching the amount of money going from the Treasury to the private domestic sector, most of which ends up as part of Commercial Bank reserves.

This means Commercial Bank reserves will not be changing much and this will not force the Central Bank's action in any significant way . The money supply being increased or decreased is controlled by the Central Bank, not by Treasury actions forcing the Central Bank's hand.

However, when Open Market Operations were the way interest rates were controlled, there was a way Treasury actions could influence the total amount of reserves required. But the effect was not opposite to Treasury spending. Instead, the effect is to change Central Bank spending in the same direction as Treasury spending. That is, Treasury spending can increase the total amount of money required to be held by the Commercial Banks. This would occur if, as a result of government spending, there was an increase in incomes, leading, through a combination of increased incomes and increased loans dispensed, to an increase in the total size of bank deposits. Since the required reserve is a percent of total bank deposits, having increased bank deposits means the amount of money required to be held as reserves goes up by the same fraction. In such a case the Central Bank would have to increase the money supply to keep the federal funds rate from rising and possibly choking off this increase in spending and incomes that was occurring in the private economy.

This case just described is a scenario where increased Treasury spending may cause the Central Bank to **increase** the money supply, opposite of the allegation that increased Treasury spending causes a need to decrease the money supply. That would have been in the past, prior to 2008.

Prior to 2008 the Central Bank may have decreased the money supply and caused an increase in interest rates to slow the economy because it was viewed as overheating, causing a risk of increased wages and inflation. It may also be true that at times government spending was playing a role in contributing to a stimulus effect on the economy, and the Central Bank is responding in part to that. But it was the Central Bank that was doing those actions based on its own independent reasons not because it was responding directly and automatically to Treasury spending.

By the way, in theory, increased Treasury spending can occur with the same size base money supply by increasing the velocity of spending of that money supply. The Treasury could tax or borrow more and spend more, meaning the same money could be circulated over and over. If the money was used to pay for non-financial real assets then the effect of all this extra spending may be to cause an increase in the size of the non-monetary real wealth supply. Presuming this does not obligate an increase in the money supply, one could imagine this spending using the same money, and the real wealth creation it causes, could continue, theoretically, without limit.

In the United States since around 2008, due to a law enacted in 2006, there was a major change to monetary policy. At that point what is known as the federal funds rate no longer became determined by the Central Bank changing the size of the money supply. Since that time interest rates are determined by the rate of interest paid to Commercial Banks by the Central Bank, on their reserves. Up until then, there was no interest paid to Commercial Banks on their reserves.

At that time, the size of excess reserves dramatically increased. The size of the Commercial Bank excess reserves increased from what used to be several billions of dollars, to trillions of dollars, that is, the size of excess reserves became orders of magnitude higher than what it used to be. This was due to a combination of paying interest on excess reserves and the implementation of something called Quantitative Easing (QE), which was a policy of creating large amounts of money. The QE increased the money supply, and paying interest on excess reserves creates resistance to decreasing it, because the more reserves a Commercial Bank has, the more interest they receive from the Central Bank.

One needs to understand that having a system where the Commercial Banks get paid interest on excess reserves is a new way and it renders using Open Market Operations, to control interest rates, obsolete.

Also important in this whole issue is what the effect of government borrowing is. Over time, government borrowing increases the debt burden. The debt burden is the percent or amount of current income needed to make payments on current debt. MMT proponents, based on their interpretations of the "Sectoral Balances" concept believe increased Treasury debt is necessary to have economic growth in the private sector. I will show later how, according to my model, this assertion is false.

When the **CENTRAL BANK** obtains money by selling assets, the money just obtained no longer exists in the money supply. It no longer needs to exist for Central Bank purposes. This means when the Central Bank obtains ownership of some money it may be considered as destroyed. But when the Treasury gets money from taxes or borrowing or earning it, the Treasury does NOT destroy it. But because the standard definition of the base money supply considers money owned by the Treasury to be out of the money supply, then spending by the Treasury will be said to put money into, and increase the size of, the money supply. People will then think there is no difference in what happens to money whether it becomes owned by the Central Bank or owned by the Treasury. In either case they will say the money upon becoming owned by either the Central Bank or the Treasury is considered out of the money supply. And that spending by either causes the money supply to increase. If one accepts that definition of the money supply, the one that says Treasury owned money is not in the money supply, this puts the ability to control the size of the money supply in the purview of both the Treasury and the Central Bank.

The reality is, the Treasury does not control money creation. The fact that the Treasury can own money and when it spends, the money used for spending becomes owned by other entities is not the same thing as creating money. The Treasury cannot declare money as existing or order its physical creation. Only the Central Bank can. This means if the Treasury is going to spend, it needs to acquire money that already exists in order to be able to spend. In that respect the Treasury is like entities in the private economy and NOT like the Central Bank. This is part of my reasoning for including money owned by the Treasury in the definition of the base money supply.

As previously mentioned, reserves held at the Central Bank make up a large part of Commercial Bank reserves, and also includes Treasury reserves and a small contribution by reserves of Fannie, Freddie, or Ginnie. This money can be virtual money (using my definition of virtual money, see "Enlightened Capitalism: A Keynes Primer") or physical money (coins and notes).

Reserves can switch back and forth, from being Commercial Bank reserves to being Treasury reserves. Payments by entities in the private domestic sector to the Treasury, such as what occurs with taxing and borrowing causes the ownership of that money to go to the Treasury. Treasury spending causes that money to become part of Commercial Bank reserves.

Central Bank spending (paid for by money created out of thin air) will increase money owned by entities other than the Treasury and when such entities get taxed or buy government bonds, that new money can become owned by the Treasury.

If a Treasury had no debt, and got all its funding from taxes, it is possible that the Treasury could build up a supply of money that steadily increased, drawing more and more money away from Commercial Bank reserves. In that way the Treasury **not spending** might cause reduced Commercial Bank reserves and lead to increased interest rates (under the old Open Market Operations system).

(Keynes called these "sinking funds", saving for a rainy day.)

But if a Treasury had to borrow to pay for its spending, then it would have the need for that money right away and will be spending it right away. The Treasury will not be borrowing money just to put the cash in storage. This means that when the Treasury taxes or borrows, that money is transferred to the ownership of the Treasury, which increases the Treasury reserves and decreases private reserves, all true, but all that is immediately reversed when the Treasury spends that money causing those reserves to be transferred right back to being part of Commercial Bank Reserves. This means that the Treasury, unless they are in a position to never borrow, in effect, does not control or change the size of the Commercial Bank Reserves. Physical money owned by private entities that are not put in banks are a bit of a wildcard because that money does not become part of Commercial Bank reserves and would not affect interest rates under the old Open Market Operations.

There are debts the Treasury acquires that might otherwise have become sinking funds, in the US, if we were not a net debtor nation. Social Security is often thought of as a place where money is sequestered and stored from money acquired from taxation, until it is eventually given to beneficiaries. But rather than existing as sinking funds it is likely that the actual money becomes used for spending like any money obtained as income for the government, and, when spent, becomes a debt for the Treasury, owed to the "Social Security Trust Fund", which it also helps to administer. It is just a question of how one is going to do the accounting. The same situation could apply to things like federal pensions.

In my definition of the base money supply, whether the Treasury is in a position to store up money or not, whether the Treasury needs to borrow or not, the Treasury never changes the overall size of the money supply. Treasury actions like spending or borrowing or taxing will not change the size of the base money supply. The same amount of money, adding together all the reserves owned by both private and government institutions will still exist in the same amount. Treasury actions may cause the ownership of a given amount of money to change, but not the total amount of reserves. Treasury actions do not change the total amount of money. Only the Central Bank increases or decreases the money supply.

But it is a little more complicated than that. We must remember that debt obligations like MBS and Treasury Bonds are not only always being purchased by the Central Bank, increasing the money supply and the Central Banks balance sheet, but the debt obligations are also always being paid off, reducing the size of the balance sheet and the money supply. So, if the Central Bank "does nothing" as these debt obligations get paid off the money supply and the balance sheet will both be constantly shrinking.

This means that to manage the money supply the Central Bank needs to be constantly active. If they want to be increasing the money supply they need to create enough money to match the amount by which the money supply is decreasing from the debt payments, and then create more money on top of that. Or if they want the money supply to be decreasing but decreasing at a rate slower than the debt payments would cause, they will need to be increasing the money supply but not as fast as the debt payments are causing the money supply to shrink.

The *effective* money supply can be reduced by money hoarding, that is, privately owned or foreign owned domestic money kept out of the banks and stored, or theoretically if it ever happened, Treasury money not used for spending. But the actual money supply is controlled by the Central Bank.

Before interest was paid on excess reserves Commercial Banks would never be part of that money hoarding because they would only earn interest if they loaned out the money they owned, (other than the money they had to keep to meet their required reserves obligation).

But now since they are paid interest on reserves, especially excess reserves, they are incentivized to own as much money as possible, whether acquired from depositors or from other sources. If they can loan that money for an interest rate higher than the IOER rate (Interest On Excess Reserves rate), then they will. But if they cannot, they have the option of just holding that money and collecting interest from the Central Bank.

Since the implementation of IOER, especially since it was combined with quantitative easing, the base money supply has grown so massive that the effect of changing the size of the money supply has changed completely, with it basically having no effect at all on the federal funds rate.

The Central Bank considers interest on reserves to be part of its operating expenses. When it pays for operating expenses, the Central Bank uses money earned as interest from assets on its balance sheet

Even though that money should be temporarily considered out of the money supply as soon as it is paid to the Central Bank, when the recipients of any of that spending on operating expenses receive that money as income it is back in the money supply. And even after all the operating expenses are paid for, any of that interest money left over is given to the Treasury, and so all of the interest payments to the Central Bank, in essence, remain in the base money supply, because all those interest earnings end up back in the possession of entities other than the Central Bank.

Note that any IOER paid to Commercial Banks for reserves, especially excess reserves, is money that would have otherwise become owned by the Treasury. This means the Treasury, (in essence, meaning taxpayers), pays for any IOER paid to Commercial Banks.

One thing I remind readers about, from "Enlightened Capitalism: A Keynes Primer", is that when a person puts money in a bank deposit that depositor comes to own an asset and the Commercial Bank comes to own the money. The depositor can control the spending of that amount of money, but the Commercial Bank owns it. Most base money put into the private sector gets put in banks so most money exists as reserves owned by the depository institutions, who have a debt obligation to the depositor as a result.

An alternative model for managing currency

Here is a model for an economy that MMT proponents mentioned in their book "Macroeconomics". In this model the Treasury serves as both Treasury and Central Bank, providing all the services each normally provide separately. In this system money owned by the "government" is created at the time it is spent and as soon as it gets reacquired as taxes or as repayment of a loan it is destroyed. Government spending is paid for with money just created in whatever amount the government deems necessary.

"In Box 9.1, we illustrate the argument that fiat currencies have value, despite not being backed by precious metal, by reference to the use of paper currency in colonial Virginia in the late 18th century."[1]

Due to a shortage of money that was hurting the ability of people to conduct commerce, the colony created its own currency. It put it into circulation by spending. It either loaned the new money (purchased a debt obligation) or used it to purchase goods and services. The recipients of that money spending then gained it as income. The money was then able to be used for further spending by those recipients, giving the economy a good currency for conducting commerce. Eventually the money would have to be paid to the government of the colony either as taxes, or as repayment for the loan the government gave them. The money must be paid back, either as the paper money, or by paying the government with British coins made of precious metals, gold and silver. Whatever the situation was, the colonial government accepted this government created money as payment of the taxes or payment for the debt obligations

When the government reacquired the money, other than any British coins, it was destroyed. The government did not save it and use it for future spending since that was not necessary. It was not necessary because whenever the colony's government needed more money for spending, they simply printed more. There was no need to keep the money obtained from taxes, or from repayment of loans owed to the government.

MMT uses this to illustrate how "taxes are not necessary to fund the government spending". According to MMT proponents,

---

1   Mitchell, William; L. Randall Wray; Martin Watts. Macroeconomics (Kindle Locations 5248-5249). Macmillan Education UK. Kindle Edition.

this example illustrates that a government that prints its own money need not tax to get money for spending. They can simply print it as needed. They also use this example to suggest that for governments who create their own money, there are no limits on how much money it can spend. As they put it, governments who create their own money are not "spending constrained".

And that is how it would work if the "government" could print all the money it wanted and spend it any way they wanted, giving it as income or benefits to whoever they wanted or purchasing debt obligations from anyone they wanted.

There are some similarities to our current fiat money system. When the colony's government spends, this immediately creates money and puts it in the money supply, similar to what happens with our current Central Bank. When the colony's government reacquires the money, it is immediately destroyed. This is also similar to when the Central Bank reacquires money making it no longer in the money supply. The distinction is the limitations on what the Central Bank is allowed to purchase with its spending, and the separation of the Central Bank and its money creation authority from the Treasury. These limitations do not apply to the colony's government.

I believe it is essential that we keep the function of the Central Bank to be one where only it can create base money, by creating and spending fiat money, but ONLY spending it on a very narrow set of assets, such as Treasury bonds and MBS. At the same time, it is essential that we make sure that the Treasury is not allowed to create money. This distinction makes all the difference in the world in allowing our economy to function successfully.

Other than the very restricted list of things the Central Bank buys and sells, mainly to control the money supply, the Central Bank is not in charge of government spending. Government institutions including any federal, state or local institutions control government spending. But none of them can create money, and therefore they need to first acquire that money, usually by taxing or borrowing, before they can spend. The need to tax or borrow to get money for spending helps keep the politicians accountable to the taxpayers, who are not only on the hook for paying taxes, but eventually also for paying off the debt.

Fortunately for us, when our banking system was designed there were wise heads around who understood the dangers of a system like they had in the Virginia colony. People who understood the need to keep authority for money creation separate from the politicians.

In our fiat system where we have a Central Bank and a Treasury, the Treasury cannot fund its spending simply by creating more money. This is true because, simply put, it does not have the right to do so!! The need for the Treasury to obtain funds by taxing and borrowing helps keep the politicians more honest and they need to consider costs. This is a way to keep funding directed to ventures that give the most benefit, overall. All this supports private sector employment and productivity by not allowing politicians to simply spend as a way to bribe voters for the purpose of keeping power. The need to tax or borrow to gain money for Treasury spending requires the government spending produce some benefit and that people who gain income from government spending perform some useful function at some point in time, present, past or future.

One could create a system like they had in the colonies. In such a system the leaders and politicians, other than out of the goodness of their own heart, would have no pressure to spend wisely or limit what they pay for. Even if no debts were paid or taxes were collected, they could still create money and spend. This "easy money" would also mean that taxpayers and borrowers would have less pressure to earn the money needed to make those payments to the Treasury. Why would the politicians strain themselves to get people to pay taxes, or why would the politicians even think of borrowing if they controlled the printing press and could just create whatever amount of money they wanted. It would not be hard to imagine that such a system could, and probably would quickly break down and no longer be viable. I imagine it would destroy democracy and the country would turn into a totalitarian state, with all the inefficiencies and poverty such systems tend to create, not to mention human suffering in general.

Fortunately, in our current system, politicians do not have that option since they don't control the money supply. Only the Central Bank can create money and it cannot spend money on whatever it wants. In fact, whenever the Central Bank creates and spends money no one in the private domestic economy or Treasury gets any increase in wealth. The money goes to asset holders in exchange for assets those asset holders already owned. In that transaction, only the Central Bank, by owning assets gets any increase in wealth. But the increase in wealth is irrelevant to the Central Bank, because, as mentioned, it can create money any time they need.

The only relevance assets on its balance sheet have to the Central Bank is it can sell those assets to reduce the money supply. It also uses the interest earned on those assets to pay for operating expenses. But since all that money becomes owned by entities other than the Central Bank, it ends up back in the money supply. It is really just a way to have those with a debt obligation to the Central Bank, mainly the Treasury, pay for Central Bank operating expenses.

There is another point I wish to make:

When money was all gold standard money (a form of what is called representative money) if a person came to own some of that money, the Central Bank had to possess a designated amount of gold in storage backing that representative money. Supposedly the owner of the money could present it to the Central Bank, trading it in for the actual gold. This meant that the amount of money owned was a debt of gold to the owner of that money.

After the 1930s or so, people were no longer allowed to trade in their gold standard currency, and receive actual gold for it. Despite that, it was still considered gold standard money, that is, it was still considered backed by gold and the Central Banks were still expected to physically possess that amount of gold in storage somewhere. The main reason they stopped allowing people to trade in their money for gold was because this was a time when, before fiat money, shortages of money could negatively impact spending. So they needed to make sure that the amount of gold owned by the Central Banks and available to be considered gold backing the money supply, was maximized.

Any time the Central Bank creates money, it gains an asset recorded on its balance sheet. An example being when a Treasury bond is purchased for the purpose of putting the money into the money supply. This is true for both fiat and gold standard money. With gold standard money, however, it would be associated with both gaining an asset and a debt. For gold standard money, any currency created must be tied to the existence of an amount of gold whose value is equivalent to the face value of that currency. And this was considered a debt of the Central Bank to the holder of the gold standard note. This remained true, even after they stopped allowing the money to be traded in for that gold. This debt caused the total amount of currency to be listed as a debt on the Central Banks balance sheet.

On the other hand, for fiat money, the Central Bank has no debt to anyone when it creates money. It does, however, get an asset on its balance sheet. Net gain of an asset on its balance sheet and no associated debt. Despite now having fiat money, money is still listed as being a debt for the Central Bank. This does not make sense, and in my view should be corrected.

CHAPTER 4
Money Income, Wealth Income?

Net Income

IF WE DEFINE spending as the transfer of ownership of money, from one person or entity to another, for a purpose…… And we define income as the amount of money the recipients of that spending obtain in the transaction, this means that, for a given time period, all the income that is created in the whole economy equals all the spending that occurs in that economy. Net income, for the whole economy, is the amount of income they are given, minus the amount of spending done. Since, when accounting for all the spending in an economy, income equals spending, then "Net Income" must equal zero.

This is not true for the microeconomy which studies firms and individuals who clearly can have income and spending be different amounts, and therefore have a "net income" that is not equal to zero.

Money Income, Wealth Income

Spending versus Wealth

I consider spending and wealth to be different categories, needing to be calculated on different axes.

They are independent variables.

Spending is the transfer of ownership of money from one person or entity to another. The spender gives the money to the recipient of the spending, and that amount of spending becomes income for that recipient. In this model the spending we are talking about is gross spending. In other words when we are accounting for spending, we are accounting for all the spending, all the transfers of ownership of money. Spending either occurs or it does not. In the macroeconomy, there is no negative total spending, it is either zero if no spending has occurred, or some positive value if transfers of ownership of money have occurred.

The spending must be done for a purpose. That is, to acquire some good, service, some labor, or some other desired outcome. All of the above-mentioned outcomes have some value to those who spent to acquire that outcome. I consider wealth to be anything that has value.

Note well: Money itself has value, money is part of wealth, however, the *spending* of that money is not wealth, the spending of that money is the transfer of ownership of the money, and calculated on a different axis, that which I call the spending or income axis. Wealth is calculated on the wealth axis, and income is calculated on the income axis.

The spending of money does not, in and of itself, create wealth or change the level of wealth in an economy. Spending may be the reason that a particular type and amount of wealth is created, but the spending and therefore the income, is not a measure of that wealth.

Money Income, Wealth Income

If the amount of wealth created in an economy is greater than the amount of wealth depleted, destroyed, deteriorated, or depreciated, then we can say that net production of wealth is positive. Whereas if more wealth is depleted than is produced then net production of wealth is negative. So, when discussing **wealth**, we can have a net wealth change different from zero.

In the SPECIAL CASE OF LOANS, which is the purchasing of a debt obligation by the lender, overall wealth is both reduced in that a debt obligation is created, and increased by the same amount in that the lender has acquired an asset based on the value of that debt obligation. The loan has caused no overall change in the level of wealth and no change in the value of the "net production" of wealth, for that given time period. The amount of base **money** does not change from that transaction, only who owns the money used for spending has changed. Looking strictly at the base money supply, this transaction caused no change in its size, nor did it cause any change in the value of total wealth in general.

To repeat, my model says the accounting of the net production of wealth is done on the wealth axis, while the spending and therefore the income earned from that spending is calculated on the income axis. They are variables that interact and affect each other but they are still independent variables. Different levels of net production of wealth can be associated with the same amount of spending. Different levels of spending can be associated with the same amount of net production of wealth.

Spending (= income) can be associated with an amount of wealth, but the amount of spending is not a measurement of that wealth or any change in the level of wealth. We cannot know simply from an accounting of how much spending was done, what the effect was on total wealth. It is possible for a given amount of spending to be associated with a *positive* net production of wealth. It can also be associated with *zero* net production, if the amount of wealth depleted equals the amount of wealth produced. Or it can be associated with, in a given time period, *negative* net production of wealth.

Examples of periods of negative net production of wealth occurring, despite even large amounts of spending and income, might include times of war, or natural disasters when spending is occurring in large amounts, but the destruction of wealth is far greater than the production of wealth.

Most models presented in economics try to combine income and wealth production into one variable. What I am calling net production of wealth, those models call income. They also call income what I call income, the amount of money received by recipients of spending. For reasons I have explained, I do not think those models can accurately explain what is occurring in the macroeconomy. They are an attempt to explain a system that has at least 2 degrees of freedom, by creating a model that has one degree of freedom.

There is an aspect of the process of lending that should be calculated on the wealth axis that does involve a change in the level of wealth. As time goes on, interest accrues. This interest and any fees paid by the borrower are paying for the services the banks provide, and those services can, in and of themselves, be considered a form of real wealth. This involves paying for all the labor, supplies, infrastructure, and other expenses needed to keep the process of lending a viable venture. That is the part of the lending process where some wealth production and maintenance does occur.

I call the purchasing of a debt obligation, the purchasing of a "purely financial asset". Other than those things interest and fees pay for, the transaction associated with *purchasing a purely financial asset does not cause any change in the level of wealth.*

The transaction creating the loan is gross spending by the lender, to purchase a debt obligation, and it becomes *gross* income for the borrower. And, when the loan is paid back, I consider this to be the purchasing back of a purely financial asset. That means, this is spending by the borrower to buy back part or all of their loan obligation, causing income to the lender. Lending increases wealth by producing purely financial assets and decreases wealth by producing debt obligations. The overall effect is no change in the level of wealth in the whole economy. Paying back loans decreases debt obligations, increasing overall wealth that way, but reduces the size of assets whose value is based on that debt obligation, by the same amount. The overall effect of paying back loans is also no change in the level of wealth in the whole economy, except what I mentioned about fees and interest.

If lending causes no increase in net production of wealth, what purpose does it have? Why would someone sell a debt obligation in order to acquire some money?

The purpose of lending is to take money from where it is not being spent, and where it is not inspiring wealth production, and *get it in the hands of* (cause it to be owned by) someone who will spend it in a way that does lead to an increase in wealth production. That is, the purpose of lending is to facilitate an increase in the amount of spending on goods, services, labor or other desired outcomes. One could also say that the purpose of lending is to increase the Velocity of money.

Spending Creates Money Income, Wealth Production Creates Wealth Income

I would like to propose another way to look at income. Heretofore I have only looked at income as being what the recipient of spending gains when they receive the money the spender gives them, and that, accounting for all the spending in the economy, the amount of the income must always be exactly equal to the amount of the spending. As a result, spending, being just the transfer of ownership of money, does not, in and of itself, cause or measure any change in the amount of money, or the level of wealth in the macroeconomy.

However, as is sometimes pointed out, money is not the only thing that people or entities can gain as a result of commerce. Besides money, people can also gain other types of wealth. I have pointed out in "Enlightened Capitalism: A Keynes Primer" how we can account for the wealth gained or lost during a period of commerce by defining what I have called net production of wealth, which I define as wealth produced minus wealth depleted. Or simply how much wealth is increased minus how much wealth is decreased. This "net production" of wealth is the change in level of wealth that occurs for the economy as a whole.

But we can also do an accounting of spending and wealth for individual persons or entities.

The difference is that for an individual his net income acquired as a recipient of spending need not be zero, they can gain or lose more money than they spend. Adding together all the spending and all the income that spending created for the whole economy will show total spending equals total income, and so in the whole economy net income is zero. But for individuals this no longer must be the case. An individual could acquire more (less) money as income than they used for spending, causing the individuals net income to be greater (less) than zero. The income created by spending is the transfer of ownership of money. The recipient has gained income in the amount of that money. And the spender has had their supply of money reduced by that amount.

Money Income, Wealth Income

To allow us less confusion, I propose that we introduce the term *money income*. I intend to have money income be the same thing as income, but its use may make things less confusing when we are discussing microeconomic situations such as when one is talking about the income of individual people or entities. Income and *money income*, refer to income created for recipients of spending. Spending may be a factor in causing wealth production, but the only income it directly causes, and is a measure of, is *money income*.

When it comes to wealth, we can define a term *wealth income*. **Wealth income**, for the whole economy, is basically what we have heretofore called net production of wealth. But we can also use this term, **wealth income**, to apply to individual entities.

For both individual entities and the whole economy, ***wealth income*** can be a positive number, a negative number or zero. Measurements of spending are always an exact number determined by the total value of all the transfers of ownership of money being analyzed. But the valuation of wealth is not always as easily determined and can have a significant subjective component. Further, wealth valuations can be constantly changing, even when there is no change in the items of wealth being included in the calculations.

In fact, accountings of the amount of wealth need not be reported as one total value but instead can be reported as an inventory of all items of wealth possessed by an individual entity or, perhaps, existing in the whole economy. This is another way an accounting of wealth is different from an accounting of money income.

Another difference between individuals and the whole economy that occurs on the wealth axis involves purely financial assets. In the whole economy creating purely financial assets does not change the level of wealth, but the same is not true for the total wealth of an individual person or entity. This is because one individual entity can acquire a purely financial asset while a different individual entity gets the associated debt obligation, causing the *wealth income* from the creation of that purely financial asset to be different than zero for both individuals.

So, the amount of money owned in the whole economy does not change due to commerce, but for an individual the amount of money owned can change. If an individual received more money as income than they lost by spending, the amount of money they end up with would be greater. Since money is a form of wealth, this difference in the amount of money owned is included in the calculation of the individual's wealth. The wealth of an individual can include a change in the amount of money owned, along with a change in all the other forms of wealth they own. But in the whole economy, the amount of that part of wealth called base money does not change unless the Central Bank increases or decreases the money supply during that time period.

So, I have defined, **money income** and **wealth income** and made clear that they measure different things, and need to be considered independent variables. They are part of an economic model with two degrees of freedom. They may strongly influence each other, but they measure different things, and must be viewed as independent variables.

CHAPTER 5
Stock and Flow! OH NO!

WHEN PRODUCING THIS book, it was never my intention to rehash all the concepts I developed in the book "Enlightened Capitalism: A Keynes Primer". However, I feel that some concepts, already developed in that book, should be repeated here. These are concepts one needs to understand properly before one can understand my critique of the Sectoral Balances concept, and for this reason I am also repeating the material here.

In the book "Enlightened Capitalism: A Keynes Primer", I explain and show in great detail how what is called the "Fundamental Identity of National income Accounting" is incorrect and does not describe a true identity. An identity is something that is true now and will remain true under all conditions.

This "Fundamental Identity" states that, in the whole macro-economy, spending equals income equals wealth production. I explain how, when accounting for all spending in the whole economy, spending and money income are equal (that part is in fact an identity). But neither can be said to be equal to production. I explain how spending and money income are measurements of the transfers of ownership of money and are not calculations of wealth,

Stock and Flow! Oh No!

and I argue that in fact money spending is an independent variable from a change in the level of wealth and that anything measuring wealth including wealth production, must be calculated on a different axis from the spending/money income axis. Spending and income must be calculated on the spending/income axis and wealth production on a separate axis I call the wealth axis.

One application that the fundamental identity greatly influences is the three different formulas for what is referred to as gross domestic product (GDP). They are the income approach, the expenditure (spending) approach, and the (wealth) production approach. It is assumed that each formula for GDP returns totals that are equal. This is of course due to the influence of the "Fundamental Identity of National Income Accounting". Note that, when taught the fundamental identity students are taught it describes an absolute identity, a "tautology", true "by definition", leaving no room for the truth of it to be questioned.

According to my model all sorts of levels of wealth, and changes in the level of wealth can be associated with one level of spending, and all sorts of levels of spending can be associated with the same amount of change in the level of wealth. They are independent variables. If one wanted to map out the different values that spending and wealth can take, those solutions would map out, at least, a two-dimensional space.

I have pointed out why in my model the "Fundamental Identity of National Income Accounting" is not a true identity. Spending equals income, but neither equals production. An identity is something that is always true, therefore, it is not an identity.

Only putting conditions and restrictions on the values the two variables can take, will make it so that a solution for one variable uniquely determines the solution for the second variable. Mathematically such a restriction would be called a constraint and serves the purpose, in this case, of reducing a two-dimensional space to a one-dimensional space.

Stock and Flow! Oh No!

I believe that much of modern macroeconomic analysis includes attempts to define such constraints.

Stock and Flow

A popular concept in economics is the concept of stock and flow. This, properly applied, is a simple concept no one can argue with. For example, if we look at wealth, or a component of wealth or all wealth, this wealth, the total wealth we are referring to is a stock. Wealth flowing into or out of that total wealth is a flow and can contribute to a change in the level of wealth.

"The Fundamental Identity of National Income Accounting", is a macroeconomic model that applies to the whole economy, the macroeconomy. It says that changes in wealth equals income equals spending (expenditure), and this could allow people to apply the supposed macroeconomic equivalency in such a way that they treat all spending as if it were a flow of wealth causing a change in the level of total wealth (the stock) in the amount of that spending.

Anyone who knows my model knows that I repeatedly explain how when we are talking about the whole economy, spending and income are not "flows of wealth" that are changing the total level of wealth, but they are in fact simply transfers of ownership of money, from the spender to recipient of that spending (***money income*** earner) and measurements of this spending are not measurements of a change in level of wealth, or for that matter, measurements of a change in the total amount of money in the whole economy. Spending can promote wealth production, but the actual spending, the transfer of ownership of money, that amount we represent as spending, is not the calculation of

Stock and Flow! Oh No!

that wealth. The calculation of that wealth is done on a separate axis. If we are looking at the whole economy, if total wealth is the stock, then the flow is not the spending of money.

In the microeconomy we can look at money spending as causing the wealth called money to flow into or out of the total wealth of an individual person or entity and this perhaps is one reason people have difficulty with understanding how, in the macroeconomy, spending of money causes no change in the amount of money overall.

For the whole macroeconomy, the flow of wealth would be something like that which I have called net production of wealth, or I could still call it wealth income, as long as one is adding all the wealth produced and subtracting all the wealth depleted. If it was not including the whole economy, then I would call it *wealth income*, which in the **microeconomy** could include a measure of the change in the amount of money a specific entity owns.

At any rate whether you are looking at the macroeconomy or the microeconomy, and whether you are looking at all those things causing a change in the total (stock of) wealth or only some of them, the flow of wealth is something measured on the wealth axis, not something measured on the spending/money income axis. In a macroeconomic model, both flow and stock are represented by things calculated on the wealth axis, but spending, the transfer of ownership of money is not a measurement of wealth or wealth changes in the level of wealth.

Only in microeconomic models can the spending represent a change of level of wealth, but it is only describing the change in the level of money owned and in that way, can affect the total wealth of **individual entities**, but not the total amount of money in the economy. The money can be a change in the amount of money owned, and therefore the amount of wealth owned due to a flow of wealth called money away from the spender and to the recipient of the

Stock and Flow! Oh No!

spending. In the **microeconomy**, it is possible to have spending and flow of wealth be describing the same process.

In a macroeconomic model, on the other hand, wealth, the net production of wealth, or, if one prefers, wealth income are all calculated on the wealth axis not the spending/money income axis. Both flow and stock are represented by things calculated on the wealth axis.

In review, regarding an accounting of the entire macroeconomy, as I see it, a big part of the problem here is that, because of the "Fundamental Identity of National Income Accounting" people interpret money spending to cause an increase in the "the total stock of wealth" in the same amount as the spending. In a macroeconomic model, the change in the stock of wealth, is not the money spending or money income, but is the wealth income, so wealth income is the flow, and it is not the same thing as, or equal to, the amount of spending.

Sectoral Balances, a macroeconomic model I discuss later, cannot be accurately interpreted when one believes (or has a model that shows) spending is a flow of wealth that can cause a change in the total level of wealth.

The exception to the rule that, in the macroeconomy, spending does not directly cause a change in the size of the (base) money supply is spending by the Central Bank. When the Central Bank spends it is mostly for the purpose of increasing the size of the money supply. Money is a form of wealth. On the other hand, when the Central Bank sells, that action reduces the money supply. The money supply increasing and decreasing can be occurring no matter what is happening to the stock of other types of wealth.

Stock and Flow! Oh No!

As I understand it, MMT proponents like to use the term "financial wealth" or "fiscal wealth", with the way they use these terms seeming to imply that spending, the transfer of ownership of money creates wealth, but the wealth it creates is "financial or fiscal wealth".

For me there are two types of "financial or fiscal wealth". Money is one type, and the other is what I call "purely financial assets". A "purely financial asset" is basically a loan. A bank deposit is the depositor loaning money to a bank, for example, and so a bank deposit qualifies as being called a purely financial asset. The production of a purely financial asset is always accompanied by a debt obligation being created in the same amount. Therefore, the production of a purely financial asset does nothing to increase (or decrease) total wealth.

One could think of the creation of the asset as having something of value flow into the total amount of wealth, but at the same time you see the accruing of the debt obligations as wealth flowing away in the same amount. Since they are both flows of equal magnitude but opposite direction, they cancel each other out so the total value of the stock of wealth is unchanged from the production of purely financial assets.

Paying off the debt obligation associated with a purely financial asset, that is, buying back that asset, has the same effect on total wealth. In that case the assets value is decreasing, wealth is flowing away, decreasing total stock of wealth. At the same time the debt obligation is decreasing, increasing the total stock of wealth, meaning wealth is flowing back into the total value of wealth. Again, the effect of each cancels the other out so paying off a purely financial asset also causes no change in size of the stock of wealth.

When spending is done to purchase a purely financial asset and its associated debt obligation, both are included in the accounting of total wealth. That is, they are accounted for on the wealth axis,

Stock and Flow! Oh No!

not the spending/income axis. The spending to pay for the resulting purely financial asset is calculated on the spending/income axis, but the value of the asset, and its associated debt obligation, are accounted for on the wealth axis. The purely financial asset is added to total wealth, and the debt obligation is subtracted from total wealth. (See prior comments on the effects of interest and fees on total wealth, hint: they increase it).

An interesting thing to mention here is that the money supply does not necessarily have to be increased to increase the amount of purely financial assets and debt obligations. Purely financial assets and debt obligations could continue to be created using the same money over and over and over to buy those assets whose value is based on debt obligations. It is spending that creates the purely financial asset. The one who acquires the asset does so by purchasing a debt obligation from the seller. But the money used to purchase the debt obligation does not necessarily stay with the seller of that debt obligation. The money can move on and be used for further spending. But for each purely financial asset created, the asset and debt obligation remain. The number of and total value of the assets and debt obligations can keep increasing, even though, since they increase and decrease the total wealth in equal measure, total wealth does not change.

When creating a purely financial asset, the total wealth has not decreased or increased, and the amount of money in the economy has not changed at all. Meanwhile, the accounting of all the spending that has occurred in these transactions is still a calculation of the total amount of transfers of ownership of money, measured on the spending/money income axis. The total value of the spending would increase with each transaction, since it is a measurement of gross spending.

Another type of asset is what I refer to as a real asset. A real asset is something that has value in and of itself. Its value is not based on a debt obligation. Strictly speaking, fiat money is a real asset, because it has value in and of itself, but here I am referring

Stock and Flow! Oh No!

to non-monetary real assets, which I also call non-financial real assets. Non-monetary real assets that are produced will increase the level of total wealth and non-monetary real assets being destroyed will reduce the level of total wealth. The total level of wealth is the "stock" and one can think of any production of non-monetary real wealth as a flow into, and an increase of, the total stock of wealth, and any depletion of non-monetary real wealth as a flow away from and a decrease of the total stock of wealth.

Economic activity that is associated with production of non-monetary real wealth usually involves spending, but again, the spending itself is neither a measure of any increase (or decrease) in the amount of money in the economy, nor is it, in and of itself, a measure of the change in the level of wealth. In fact, even when the spending is associated with economic activity that does cause an increase in the level of non-monetary real wealth, there is no one to one correlation between the amount of spending and the type, amount, or value of the wealth created.

Since the Central Bank increasing or decreasing the money supply causes no change in the level of wealth existing outside the Central Bank, and since the creation, or paying off, of a purely financial asset also causes no change in the total level of wealth, then the only wealth measurement that matters when looking at the change in total wealth in the macroeconomy, is the measure of what is happening to non-monetary real wealth.

Conclusion:

In the macroeconomy, accounting for all transactions in the economy, it is not valid to look at money income as a flow because it does not measure any money going into and changing the total value of the entire money supply (the "stock" of money). What spending, which equals money income, measures is all the transfers of ownership of money occurring using the current money supply. In a purely macroeconomic model, only wealth income (net production of wealth) is a flow of wealth causing an increase (or decrease) in the stock of wealth for all the entities in the whole economy combined. And it is the only thing contributing to measures of changes in the level of wealth. Net money income, in the macroeconomy, equals zero and therefore spending of money and the income it creates makes no contribution to any change in the level of wealth.

The Sectoral Balances equation, which will be discussed in more detail soon, only measures base money being used for spending, where it comes from when first used for spending in that time period, and where it ends up. It is not a measure of what is happening to wealth other than that wealth we call money. It does not measure changes in the level of wealth caused by changes in the level of non-monetary real wealth, (which I also call non-financial real wealth). But I have seen that while proponents of MMT seem to recognize that measures of non-monetary or non-financial real wealth do not belong in the Sectoral Balances equation they do not treat purely financial assets the same. This is where the terms "fiscal or financial wealth" or "fiscal or financial assets" come into play. It seems that they view it as ok to include what I call purely financial assets as part of what is measured in the Sectoral Balances equation.

Since, in the macroeconomy, the effect on the stock of wealth by the creating or the paying off of purely financial assets is zero, this strategy, of including the accounting of purely financial assets in the interpretation of what the Sectoral Balances equation measures is one where they are adding zero to an equation that describes an equivalency. If you have an equation where the elements describe an equivalency and you add zero to it, it is still equal. This is true

Stock and Flow! Oh No!

even if what you are adding is a completely extraneous element that does not belong in that equation.

I can be asked for an accounting of the number of cases of apples in the warehouse and only the apples. I return with the answer that number of cases of apples = 27. I could also return with the answer that the number of cases of apples = 27 plus zero Bentleys. The equivalency stands, and strictly speaking it is still correct, but reporting there are no Bentleys in the warehouse is extraneous and serves no purpose. You can add zero of anything to an equivalency and it will still be equal, but that does not mean any purpose was served.

We cannot make up terms, like calling purely financial assets "fiscal wealth" and then hide behind the fact that there is no change of total wealth when purely financial assets are created, to allow us to include the value of those purely financial assets and associated debt obligations, in an equation where only an accounting of base money belongs.

The Sectoral Balances equation is not measuring purely financial assets, it is not measuring debt obligations, and it is not measuring any assets other than money. Trying to add these values that should be measured on the wealth axis to elements of the Sectoral Balances equation, as if they were base money or spending of base money, could give an incorrect result. One might be tempted to include the value of the purely financial asset as if it is "money income" and the value of the debt obligation as if it is spending. Doing so is an incorrect interpretation of the data. This concept is discussed more later.

Someone may try to point out that when one sector buys a purely financial asset by giving money to another sector, to purchase a debt obligation from them, this spending has caused a change in the total wealth of one sector relative to another. This is not actually true, since due to the transfer of ownership of money from the sector buying the asset to the sector agreeing to the debt obligation, each sector's total wealth remains unchanged from the transaction..

The effect of incorrectly adding measures of wealth as if they were measures of spending is an extremely important concept to understand, if one wants to fully understand this Sectoral Balances theory, as it is normally taught.

CHAPTER 6
SAVINGS

IN THE MACROECONOMY, there is income and there is savings. Savings is something that is measured on the wealth axis, but there are two parts to savings. The first part is the preservation of money used for spending in the current time period. That money continues to exist after being used for spending and ends up possessed by some entity or person who received it as *money income*. That savings is also the part of savings that equals investment in the savings equals investment identity. It is the savings that represents the preservation of the money put into spending as investment spending (see chapter 2 in my book, "Enlightened Capitalism: A Keynes Primer"). That part of savings is always money only.

Only if the Central Bank sold assets to acquire that money would that money not continue to exist, or of course it would no longer exist if it were destroyed. However, the act of spending and conducting commerce does not cause that money to be destroyed. Generally, it is preserved, continues to exist, remains in the money supply, and is owned by some person or entity in the economy.

This money circulates though the economy with people or entities earning it as *money income*. The recipients of this income, in the form of money, may choose to re-spend it or not, but ultimately some entity or person who received that money as income, is left owning that money at the end of the given time period. That money is designated as "saved" and is the first part of savings. *Spending* is not wealth, but money is wealth and that part of savings, that money that is the preservation of investment, is accounted for on the wealth axis.

The second part of savings is a measurement of changes in the level of wealth, specifically it measures wealth produced minus wealth depleted, in the time period under study. For the whole economy I usually refer to this as net production of wealth, but it could also be labeled wealth income. For individual entities, a microeconomic scenario, I can only use the term wealth income.

All savings is wealth, and all savings is measured on the wealth axis. For the **macroeconomy**, this includes the money that has been put into spending which continues to exist at the end of the given time period, plus the "net production of wealth".

An *individual* could end up with positive acquisition of wealth due to acquiring and not further spending money acquired as *money income*. An individual could end up with positive acquisitions of wealth due to acquiring more purely financial assets than debt obligations. And an individual could end up with positive acquisitions of wealth by acquiring non-financial real assets, or having the value of non-financial real assets already owned increase. Any of that increased wealth gets measured on the wealth axis.

Negative change in wealth could occur for an individual by them spending more money than is received by them as *money income*. Negative changes in wealth could occur for an individual by acquiring more debt obligations than purely financial assets. Negative change in wealth could occur for an individual by having the amount or value of non-financial real assets the individual owns reduced. Any of that decrease in wealth also gets measured on the wealth axis.

CHAPTER 7
Correcting GDP

IF YOU LOOK at chapter 2 from the book "Enlightened Capitalism: A Keynes Primer", you will see the equation for total spending, Y, defined as being equal to Investment plus Consumption. I give specific definitions for Investment and for Consumption and show how the equation $Y = I + C$ is a pure measure of spending. It does not measure or have as part of its definition any component equal to wealth other than the money being used for spending during that time period. The total amount of money being used for spending in the given time period, I call Investment spending (I).

It is common in macroeconomic equations to have Y be considered a measure of total spending. Because of the "Fundamental Identity of National Income Accounting" it is generally assumed that Y must also equal the change in the level of wealth for a given time period. "The flow of wealth equals spending", economists might say.

This becomes relevant now in our discussion of GDP.

GDP, Gross Domestic Product is a proper name for wealth produced in a given time period, in a given country, and could be defined as part of the net production of wealth in that country during

Correcting GDP

that time period. It is not always a complete measure of the net production of wealth because wealth depleted is not always considered. But I just want to acknowledge that the term Gross Domestic *Product* is probably most appropriately utilized when one is measuring *production*.

However, since the standard teaching of GDP is based largely on the "Fundamental Identity of National Income Accounting" we have ended up with 3 ways to define and measure Gross Domestic Product. The 3 definitions for GDP are labeled as the Production Approach to GDP, the Income approach to GDP and the Expenditure (spending) approach to GDP. As it turns out, two of them are not really measurements of production, but are, in fact, mostly measures of spending. Generally, economists believe that when applied to the real economy, the three definitions of GDP should return equal results. If they do not, the explanation given is that this occurred only because we do not have all the necessary data. It is my view that the Income approach to GDP and the Expenditure approach to the GDP should give identical totals but that neither should reliably end up valued the same as the wealth created that the Production approach calculation returns. I assert that the real reason the production approach to GDP does not generally equal the expenditure (spending) and income approaches is because the Fundamental Identity is wrong.

Further complicating things is that the different standard definitions of GDP can be mixtures of both spending, which should be measured on the spending/money income axis, and wealth, which needs to be measured on the wealth axis. Since we should not be measuring wealth production and money spending on the same axis, we should not have definitions of GDP that are both measures of spending and wealth mixed, as though wealth and spending are measures of things in the same category. For measures of GDP to be fully accurate, they need to be pure measures of wealth, or pure measures of spending, not mixtures. Y is either measuring total spending and gross income, or it is measuring total wealth produced, or even better, net production of wealth.

Certainly, the name expenditure approach implies that spending is being measured. In "Enlightened Capitalism" I noted that the standard definition of GDP was not entirely a measure of spending or production, that it was a mix of both. I noted that to make it purely a measure of the spending, our definitions and interpretations of what the elements of the expenditure approach GDP are measuring needed to be modified. In the process I had to make a clearer definition for what economy spending and income are being measured. I addressed that issue in Chapter 30 of "Enlightened Capitalism, 2nd Edition,"

I will repeat that discussion here:[2]

"First I would like to address the issue of whether the income approach to GDP should count as the income earned in the private domestic economy only or if it should include income earned in the private domestic economy plus income earned by the government.

Government income is generally considered revenue from taxes. If one were to see GDP as a measure of spending and income, then taxes would be a transfer of ownership of money from the private sector to the government for a purpose. A toll is a tax, and you have just paid for the service of being able to cross that bridge or use that road. Similarly, property taxes pay for being allowed to live in a town and benefit from that town's services and infrastructure. Social Security taxes pay for the ability to be able get income when we either become retired or disabled. Income taxes and sales taxes pay for all the benefits we and our society gain from what the

---

2   Bright M.D., Daniel, Enlightened Capitalism: A Keynes Primer . Outskirts Press, Inc.. Kindle Edition. Location 3845 of 7961.

state, local or federal government provides. In short, taxes do count as spending because they are transfers of ownership of money for a purpose, with the purposes including causing those outcomes just mentioned, to occur.

In some descriptions of the income approach to GDP some taxes such as Sales taxes are included in GDP, but many other taxes are not. In my model, you can't do that. If the income approach to GDP is going to be a pure measure of income, (and all income), you must include all spending and not pick and choose. This means if one is going to include government income in GDP then one must include all spending that causes income to government recipients, which certainly means including all taxes but also means including other spending, which I discuss more of in the next chapter (Note: I am referring to chapter 31 of 'Enlightened Capitalism' in this part of the quote).

It is my view that including all taxes and other things that generate income for a government in our expression for the income approach to GDP would cause it to be a radical departure from what is usually included in standard definition. The standard definition is closer to what one would get by just including income occurring in the private domestic economy. Therefore, my modified definition of income approach to GDP will not include government income but will be strictly a measure of private domestic income. By a similar argument, and because in the macroeconomy spending and income are equal, my modified version of the expenditure approach to GDP will also be solely a measure of private domestic spending."

Since I am modifying the definition of GDP that means I am altering it. I am altering it for the reasons I have stated repeatedly in this book and in "Enlightened Capitalism". In deciding what needs to change I run up against issues like what is the economy that the definitions of GDP are calculating the income for. As noted here the standardly taught definition doesn't fully address that, or at least doesn't address it well.

Correcting GDP

Clearly, for the most part, the standard definition does not include Government income being part of the income GDP measures, and the format of the standardly taught expenditure approach to GDP resembles the modified version I will derive for GDP when one considers the private domestic economy to be the one whose spending and income is being measured. Even if the definitions and interpretations of the elements must be modified somewhat, the standard definition for expenditure approach to GDP has all the same elements I use in the modified expression I derive, when I consider the economy being measured to be the private domestic economy. Besides, I can only derive the Sectoral Balances equation from the modified equation for expenditure approach to GDP if the private domestic economy is the one being analyzed.

In examining the expenditure approach to GDP, we note its similarity to $Y = I + C$. We know from Chapter 2 of "Enlightened Capitalism: A Keynes Primer" that $Y = I + C$ is both a pure measure of spending, and measures all the spending occurring in the macroeconomy. If I can modify, as needed, the standardly taught equation for the Expenditure approach to GDP so that it becomes a pure measure of spending, and the spending measured accounts for all the spending and income occurring in that economy in the current time period, then that equation will be equivalent to $Y = I + C$. It will then just be a matter of determining which elements in the modified expenditure approach to GDP correlate to I and which to C. As noted, for this purpose, the macroeconomy whose income is being measured will be the private domestic economy.

The Sectoral Balances equation is derived from the expression for savings, but only the part of savings that is the preservation of money used for spending in the given time period. That is the part of spending I call investment and is the same money preserved as savings in

Correcting GDP

the expression savings equals investment. This part of savings is a true identity. It is always true at all times and for all specified time periods.

If I can use the elements of my modified version of the equation for the expenditure approach to GDP to derive the Sectoral Balances equation, and show that it is equivalent to Savings equals Investment, then that Sectoral Balances equation will also be an identity.

A Modified Equation for The Expenditure Approach to GDP

First, I will detail the derivation of a modified expression for the expenditure approach to GDP that is a pure expression of spending, without any elements describing changes in the level of wealth, either assets or debits. Much of the material here is copied from chapter 31 of my book "Enlightened Capitalism: A Keynes Primer".

In order to accomplish this, I analyzed all the elements commonly taught in the expenditure approach to GDP and made modifications to get a revised expression.

The "Y" derived from this modified expression for GDP will be a quantity measuring the total amount of transfers of ownership of money in that time period, all investment spending and all consumption spending, again with these expressions being defined as in chapter two of "Enlightened Capitalism: A Keynes Primer". It will not be a measure of wealth production, just spending.

CORRECTING GDP

Reminder:

I do not calculate spending as the "flow" of wealth. Stock and flow are things that are entirely accounted for on the wealth axis. The flow of wealth is a calculation of the amount of (usually net) wealth produced in a given time period. The stock of wealth is the amount of total wealth that exists at a given time. Neither of those values are calculated on the income or expenditure (spending) axis. The only wealth described in the Sectoral Balances equation is base money.

Spending and income are not measures of wealth or even the change in levels of wealth in the MACROECONOMY. This will therefore be true for the modified expression I will derive for the expenditure approach to GDP, in the next few pages. All the elements in that expression will be measures of base money and the transfer of ownership of that base money. This spending could theoretically be the transfer of ownership of whatever is being used as base money.

Recall that the expression from chapter two of "Enlightened Capitalism: A Keynes Primer" Y=I+C defines not just spending but all spending. Therefore, any quantity that can be shown to be contributing to the value of Y, must also be definable as being part of either I or C. Just so there is no mistake as to what I am talking about, when I am talking about the expression Y = I + C, I will be referring to I as "Keynes' I" and C as "Keynes' C". I will, over the course of the next few pages, show which parts of this modified expenditure approach to GDP are part of "Keynes' I" and which are part of "Keynes' C".

Correcting GDP

The expenditure approach to GDP is normally defined by this expression

$Y = I_p + G - T + X - M + C$

Y = private domestic income or gross domestic product

I_p = private investment

The term I_p is used here instead of I to distinguish the I_p in the formula for GDP from the I in Keynes' formula $Y = I + C$

G = government investment or purchases

T = taxes

C = consumption

X = exports

M = imports

X − M is usually put in parenthesis like (X − M) or referred to as "Net Exports" or NX. I do not put them in parenthesis for reasons that will become clear later. The expression (X − M) is referred to as a trade surplus if X>M and (X − M) is positive or as a trade deficit if X<M and (X − M) is negative.

Sometimes the expenditure approach to GDP uses the same expression without the taxes:

$Y = C + I_p + G + X - M$, although this turns out to be closer to the final equation I will derive, I wish to stick with analyzing this equation

$Y = C + I_p + G - T + X - M$

Let us analyze these elements to see where this equation for the expenditure approach to GDP does represent income. and where it may represent something that should be calculated on the wealth axis. We will also discuss what modifications are needed to make it purely a calculation of income, not wealth.

Private Investment I_p

What I call investment and what is commonly defined as investment in GDP are different things. For the expenditure approach equation to represent income, I need to have I_p represent investment spending …………..(as defined in chapter two of "Enlightened Capitalism: A Keynes Primer", spending of money being put into income for the first time in the given time period) ……….. but only that part of investment spending that is the transfer of ownership of money from private domestic entities to other private domestic entities. If, however, this spending qualified as consumption spending,……….. (as defined in chapter two of "Enlightened Capitalism: A Keynes Primer", spending paid for out of current income)……… then it will be categorized as part of C. I further elaborate on these definitions in chapter 31 of "Enlightened Capitalism: A Keynes Primer". I recommend the reader review that material as it will provide a much more thorough explanation of my reasoning for defining things as I do here.

All the spending that I have specified as qualifying to be counted as private investment, I_p, is part of Keynes' I in the expression Y = Keynes' I + Keynes' C, but I_p does not account for all the spending that will qualify as being part of Keynes' I.

Before I leave the category of private investment, I would like to talk about another difference in my model and GDP as taught. That is the issue of intermediate products. The short explanation is that spending does not get counted as part of the standard explanation of GDP if you are paying for "intermediate products". Intermediate products are not "final products" but will, after more production phases, become part of a final product. This is an attempt to make the income in GDP be "net income", and at the same time it is an attempt to equate the value of the final product with income. This concept is best explained using an example:

Correcting GDP

A unit of product in this scenario will be enough to make one loaf of bread as the end product. Suppose a farmer pays 1 dollar per unit to workers to grow wheat. The farmer sells the wheat to a flour mill for 2 dollars per unit. The mill makes flour and sells it to the baker for 3 dollars per unit. And the baker makes loaves of bread and sells them for 4 dollars per unit. Gross income, i.e., total spending equals $1 + 2 + 3 + 4 = 10$ dollars per loaf of bread produced, but the final product is worth only 4 dollars.

In the standard way the expenditure approach to GDP is taught, they only consider what is paid for the end product to count as part of income. They do not count any income earned for making what they call "intermediate products". This is perfectly appropriate if the expenditure approach to GDP were to describe the value of production in the given time period. As I am modifying the expenditure approach to be a measure of income, and since Keynes' $Y = I + C$, is a measure of gross spending and income, spending for intermediate products must be included as part of Keynes' I or Keynes' C. In the example given, the gross spending and income that occurs as a result of making a loaf of bread is 10 dollars, not 4 dollars. Again, Y = Keynes' I plus Keynes' C is measuring gross income, not net income.

Let us go to the next element of $Y = I_p + G - T + C + X - M$

G Government Spending

In standard teaching, G means government spending. In the standard definition of expenditure approach to GDP G includes government spending on goods and services needed to run the government, and government spending paid to support producing and maintaining public capital goods. G includes paying for infrastructure production and maintenance, and G also includes paying for schools, law enforcement, military, medical care and all the other things that you can imagine must be paid for by government.

Correcting GDP

What is excluded from G in the standard model is what are referred to as government transfers like unemployment, food stamps, social security etc. Since this is the transfer of ownership of money for a purpose, in my model it is part of spending and income, and therefore must be included in the expenditure approach to GDP if it is going to be a true measure of all income. Therefore, I include the government transfers as part of G.

As a technical point, I categorize all government spending as part of Keynes' investment (Keynes' I). We know that all components of GDP must be categorizable as either Keynes' Investment or Keynes' Consumption (Keynes' C) because GDP = Y = Keynes' Investment plus Keynes' consumption, and because Y represents all spending. This also means that all spending that qualifies as Keynes' investment (according to my definitions) is accounted for somewhere in the components of GDP and all spending that qualifies as Keynes' consumption is also accounted for somewhere in the components of GDP.

Any income earned by the government, as a result of spending directed at the government (like, for example, taxes), does not count as private domestic income. It is government income. The modified expenditure approach to GDP equation is a calculation of total private domestic income, not government income. Keynes' consumption is spending paid for out of current private domestic income, i.e., current GDP. But because any money received by the government creates government income and not private domestic income, then the source of money paid by the government (G) to create income in the private domestic sector cannot have been private domestic income. This means government payments, G, do not qualify to be considered Keynes' C, since they are not directly paid for out of current private domestic income.

We know from chapter 2 of "Enlightened Capitalism", that Keynes' consumption and Keynes' investment' are complementary, i.e., they account for all spending in the private domestic economy, and that they are mutually exclusive, that is, if some private domestic income is paid for by spending considered Keynes' consumption it cannot be Keynes Investment. But if some private domestic income is caused by spending that does not meet the definition for Keynes' consumption it MUST BE Keynes' investment spending.

Government spending may or may not be paid for out of current government income, but that does not matter. Government spending is not paid for out of current private domestic income; therefore, it does not count as consumption in GDP. Since it does not count as consumption then it must count as investment spending, therefore, in the expenditure approach to GDP all government spending G is categorized as part of Keynes' investment, i.e., part of Keynes' I.

Another way to look at this is using the savings equals investment identity. Any money the government does **not** pay to some entity in the private domestic economy will not exist at the end of the given time period as savings owned by some private domestic entity and will NOT be added to the savings that is the preservation of investment, preservation of "Keynes' I". But any money the government does pay to private domestic entities, will exist at the end of the given time period, owned by some entity in the private domestic economy and become part of the private domestic savings that is the preservation of investment. (Unless of course it was removed again prior to the end of the given time period such as by taxes, reviewed next). Since that is part of the savings that equals investment, then it must logically follow that government spending should be considered investment, as part of Keynes' I. That is why government spending is best characterized as investment spending. In my model, when modifying the expenditure approach to GDP to be a true measure of income, G will always be considered part of Keynes' I.

$$Y = I_p + G - T + C + X - M$$

Next, We Look at T, i.e., Taxes

Correcting GDP

GDP is a measure of private domestic income; it does not include government income. Taxes are spending by private domestic sector entities targeted at becoming income for the government. Taxes are a transfer of ownership of that money from the private domestic sector to the government.

In the expenditure approach equation for GDP, taxes are sometimes listed as having to be subtracted off private domestic income. As it turns out, it is not valid to include taxes that way. If that equation is going to be considered a measure of gross private domestic income, it is incorrect to have the expression -T be part of the expenditure approach to GDP. Here is why:

After the tax money has become owned by the government it is no longer available to be used for spending by entities in the private domestic economy. One might assume that because that money is no longer available to be used for private domestic spending that it has reduced private domestic spending by the same amount and should be subtracted off the income, meaning that taxes should remain an element in GDP. That is incorrect. This is because the effect of taxes cannot be to undo spending that has already occurred. We cannot subtract taxes off the totals for spending that we get from other elements in GDP, such as I_p, and C because those are totals of spending that have already occurred. The effect of taxes is to influence the amount of spending that will occur. The effect of taxes is to influence what the values of I_p, G, and C will be, not to subtract off what they already are. The effect of taxes is already baked into the values of I_p, G, C, and even X.

We do not know how much taxes will reduce the total spending, however. If taxes were taken from money that was not intended to be spent, then it may have no effect on the value of the components of GDP. If, in the time period under analysis, taxes prevent the one time spending of a given amount of money from occurring, spending that would otherwise have occurred and occurred only one time, then they have stopped that money from being put into income at all and that will lower total spending dollar for dollar. In that case there is a correlation between taxes and private investment spending. If, however, the taxes remove money that has already been put into spending, money that someone has already received as income, then we do not know how it will affect total income, because we do not know how it will affect further consumption spending. So, for example, it could have been that had that money not been removed from the private domestic economy it still would have been spent multiple times over, in which case the reduction in total income would be greater than the amount of the taxes. Also, Taxes could affect the level of government spending G in that if more taxes are collected it might make more government spending possible. Or taxes can affect the price of exports, changing the amount of exports sold. So, the reality is, we do not know if taxes will result in a lot less spending, a little less spending, no change in spending or even more spending. Taxes certainly can influence the amount of spending, but they should not be included in the GDP formula as subtracted off. There should not be a -T in the formula for GDP.

The effect of taxes on that part of savings that is the preservation of investment is different, however. Taxes taking money out of the private sector means that any sum of money that had become used for spending in the private domestic sector, which is then used to pay taxes, will not remain in the private domestic sector. Using that money to pay taxes will reduce the amount of money that ends up preserved as savings in the private domestic sector. That money will still exist, just "saved" in the government's pocket instead of being owned by someone in the private domestic sector. Overall, the savings equals investment identity holds, it is just that some of that saved money is not existing in private domestic hands anymore, it is saved in government hands.

The contribution of taxes to the savings equals investment identity changes the equation of the relationship between savings and investment (not including net production) so that the savings equals investment identity becomes: "Private Domestic Savings equals Keynes' Investment minus any taxes paid for by current private domestic income".

Taxes that prevented investment spending from occurring in the first place (i.e., taxes that remove money from the private sector before it gets used for any spending in the given time period), do not affect the savings equals investment formula because that money was never part of investment spending and never contributed to any income and would not be part of what we consider the savings that is preservation of investment. It is only if the taxes take money that has already been used for spending and has created income for some private domestic entity, out of the private domestic economy, i.e., by getting the money out of the active spending and into government coffers, that the savings equals investment identity would be affected. This is why the equation for savings (not including the part of savings that is net production) turns into "savings equals investment minus taxes paid for out of current private domestic income".

There is something related to taxes that we should discuss here. Taxes are income to the government. They are spending by the private domestic sector directed at the government as the recipient of that spending. There is another thing that I include as "spending by the private domestic sector directed at and creating income for the government". In my model, the government borrowing from the private domestic sector counts as income for the government. That is, it counts as spending by the private domestic sector to buy an asset from the government (Treasury note, savings bond, whatever). In that case the government is selling a loan obligation to the private domestic sector. The spending by the private domestic sector to buy that asset becomes income for the government. However, since it is spending directed at the government it is income for the government and not the private sector. Therefore, it is not counted as part of the expenditure approach to GDP. Its effect on GDP is similar to taxes, that is, it influences the values the other components of GDP take, but the amount of borrowing by the government does not get subtracted off of GDP.

The difference between taxes and government borrowing is how Government spending G is affected and the effect that has on the multiplier. With taxes the government is free to spend the money how it wishes. With borrowing, in the future, not only will the money have to be paid back to the private lenders (bondholders etc.), but interest will be paid to them as well.

The investors in government bonds will, on the average, tend to be wealthier. This means that when the government is paying off bonds with interest one would expect the multiplier effect of money being paid to those wealthier bond holders will be lower than the multiplier effect of other government spending in general. The reason is because one would expect that a larger fraction of other government spending, not including paying off government debt, would be targeted at programs that accrue proportionately more benefit to lower income people.

In the category of taxes, we need to include any transactions where the private domestic sector buys anything from the government, any item of wealth including goods and services the government can provide, as well as paying for debt obligations from the government, and any taxes paid. When I refer to Taxes, T, in this discussion, I include any payment from the private domestic economy to the Government.

Correcting GDP

I have discussed in detail the role of taxes in GDP and have concluded that the expenditure approach equation for GDP cannot validly include the term (-T), i.e., minus taxes, as an element.

Because of how we must handle taxes this $Y = I_p + G - T + C + X - M$ .... the expenditure approach to GDP becomes:

$Y = I_p + G + C + X - M$

In addition, as regards savings, if we exclude net production, the expression for savings in the private domestic sector becomes:

Private Domestic Savings equals Keynes' Investment minus any taxes paid for from current income.

Moving to other elements of $Y = I_p + G - T + C + X - M$

We next look at exports minus imports aka (X - M), also referred to as NX which stands for net exports.

This category may seem straightforward and obvious, especially to people who have been seeing it mentioned in economic textbooks and papers and economics statistics for years. X stands for exports and is spending by a foreign entity aimed at becoming income in the domestic economy. The spending to pay for the exports, must be considered investment. It cannot be consumption because to be consumption it must be paid for by money acquired as part of private domestic income. Since the money used for buying the domestic economy's exports is paid for by money from a foreign economy it cannot be paid for with money acquired as current domestic income. Therefore, spending to pay for exports will be classified as investment spending, like government spending is. X is part of private domestic income and is included as part of Keynes' Investment spending.

M stands for imports. Imports are paid for by transferring ownership of money from our private domestic economy to foreign entities. It is spending targeted at creating income for a foreign entity. It is not creating income for any entities in the private domestic economy. The spending to pay for imports does not get subtracted off the total for GDP. Like taxes, the effect of spending to purchase imports is not to undo private domestic spending that has already occurred, but to affect the amount of spending that will occur. Again, we do not know exactly how this spending on imports will affect domestic spending. It may reduce it a lot, a little, or not at all. And it is even possible that the imports will spark more domestic spending. Imports may be raw materials that are used for production in the private domestic economy, which leads to more jobs and production, and more spending. Or just the presence of the imports may spark desire for other products, leading again to more production, jobs and spending. Or, just the re-selling of the imports may draw out extra investment spending or consumption spending. As I said, we do not know the effect of imports on total income, but we do know that, like taxes, the effect of spending on imports is already baked into the value of the other elements of GDP. There should not be a term "-M", i.e., minus imports, in the expenditure approach equation for GDP.

If we ignore the portion of savings that is net production, the effect of imports on savings is like taxes. Any money acquired from current income used to pay for imports will be subtracted from private domestic savings. Any spending using money that had not already been used for spending in the current time period will not have been part of domestic spending at all and therefore, does not get subtracted off savings.

The savings equal investment identity when imports are considered is savings equals Keynes' investment minus any spending to acquire imports paid for out of current private domestic income.

The savings equals investment identity when both taxes and imports are considered becomes:

Correcting GDP

Savings equals Keynes' investment minus any taxes or imports paid for by money acquired as current private domestic income.

There is one thing I should mention about the relationship of savings and imports. When deciding what counts as paying for imports, we do not just include money paid for items that will physically be transported to the domestic country, nor do we just pay for services utilized by private domestic entities while physically located in the domestic country. We may also include, as part of M, spending to acquire items from foreign entities that stay in a foreign country. Any money spent to pay for something acquired from a foreign country will be money that has left the private domestic economy and will no longer be available to be counted as part of the savings that is the preservation of investment. That money will no longer be owned by, and considered savings for, anyone in the private domestic economy, at the end of the given time period.

Getting back to the equation for the expenditure approach for GDP we have shown it should not include "minus taxes" (-T) or "minus imports" (-M). We now understand that the equation for GDP should be $Y = I_p + G + X + C$ with the idea that taxes and imports can affect the values of the other variables, but the effect is already contained in the reported values of I_p, G, X, and C.

Next, we look at C

In the standardly taught definition of GDP, C stands for consumption. Since the production approach to GDP focuses on production occurring in the current time period, and since the "Fundamental Identity" says all the different formulas for GDP should give the same result, then it is reasonable to infer that the consumption in the standardly taught expenditure approach to GDP formula also focuses on things purchased in the current time period. This is not always the case, as I can find several definitions of consumption that don't focus on that issue. This is not really an issue for the purposes of this book, since my definition is specific and the one we will be using. But assume the standard way to look at it is that consumption is buying things made in the current time period produced by the private domestic economy. The Standardly taught approach puts no restrictions on what money can be used for the purchases. The spending can be paid for by money earned in a previous time period or money earned in the current time period. The items bought also have certain definitions and restrictions that can vary. Which is also not important since my definition does not focus on what is bought.

I have an opposite interpretation for what C needs to be to correlate with Keynes' C:

First, C needs to be restricted to that spending which is paid for out of some private domestic entity's current income, and second, consumption includes purchases of things……. (goods, services, labor, any other desired outcome) ……..produced in any time period, including the future, and by anyone, ….. (including, by the way, things produced by nature)…… as long as the payment is to some other person or entity in the private domestic economy. "Consumption" paid for by money not earned as part of current income, counts as part of Keynes' I, i.e., I_p, it is not part of Keynes' C. My definitions make clear what spending is investment and what is consumption. In comparing Keynes' equation $Y = I + C$ to the expenditure approach to GDP as modified in this chapter, then the C in this GDP equation has the same meaning as Keynes' C whereas Keynes' $I = I_p + G + X$.

Y = Keynes' I + Keynes' C becomes $Y = (I_p + G + X) + C$

The Modified Expenditure Approach to GDP is $Y = I_p + G + X + C$

This makes this modified expenditure approach to GDP completely correlate to Keynes' Y = Keynes' I + Keynes' C and be solely a measure of spending and (money) income.

Correcting GDP

This concludes my analysis of the expenditure approach to GDP and my comments on what modifications we need to make in collecting our data so that it will be a true measure of total spending = demand = gross income.

⸎

Now that we have defined what Keynes' I would be in our modified definition for the expenditure approach to GDP the expressions for the savings that is preservation of investment becomes:

When taxes are considered:

Savings equals Keynes' I minus any taxes paid for out of current income, that is Savings equals (I_p + G + X) minus any taxes paid for out of current income.

Similarly, the savings equal investment identity when imports are considered becomes:

Savings equals (I_p + G + X) minus any spending to acquire imports paid for out of current income.

The savings equals investment identity when both taxes and imports are considered becomes:

Savings equals (I_p + G + X) minus any taxes or imports paid for by money acquired as current income.

So here, both taxes paid for out of current income and imports paid for out of current income get subtracted off of savings, but no part of T or M gets subtracted off the modified expression for the expenditure approach to GDP.

Note that if taxes or imports are paid for out of money that has not been put into spending at all yet (targeted at private domestic entities) and has not been received as part of current private domestic income, that money will not be subtracted off the savings that is preservation of investment. The reason is that the spending was targeted at recipients that were outside of the private domestic economy, such as foreign entities or the government, but the money used was never received as part of anyone's private domestic income, it would never have become part of Keynes' investment and would not be eligible to be part of the savings that is preservation of investment.

The money that was put into spending as investment is preserved, even in an economy that interacts with the government and interacts with foreign economies. It is just that some of that money may end up being owned by the government or foreign entities, and not by entities in the private domestic economy.

CHAPTER 8
SECTORAL BALANCES

I HAVE SHOWN a way to make the expenditure approach to GDP into an expression that is totally a measure of spending. And how the identity savings equals investment fits in using the definitions for investment and savings I developed in chapter two of "Enlightened Capitalism: A Keynes Primer"

So, we have this expression:

Savings equals (I_p + G + X) minus any taxes or imports paid for by money acquired as current income.

Where T does not just stand for taxes but stands for any payment from private domestic entities to the government including taxes, payments for bonds, and any purchases of items of wealth from the government

IF we make the proviso that all of T is paid for out of current income, and we also assume that all imports (M) are paid for out of current income, then this equation can be reduced to

Savings equals (I_p + G + X) minus T minus M.

Or

Sectoral Balances

Savings $(S) = I_p + (G - T) + (X - M)$

Which can be written $(S - I_p) + (T - G) + (M - X) = 0$

This expression is the equation Modern Monetary Theory refers to as the Sectoral Balances equation. Their idea is that this equation describes the income minus the spending by 3 sectors, the private domestic sector, the government sector, and the foreign sector, where S, T, and M represent the income earned by those sectors and I_p, X and G represent the spending by those sectors.

What this expression really looks at is where the money used for spending during that time period came from and ends up. The expression says that the money that was put into spending for the first time in the private domestic economy during this time period ("Keynes Investment", i.e., $[I_p + G + X]$), gets saved and will still exist as owned by entities in the private domestic economy (S), except for that money which leaves the private domestic economy to be owned by the government (T) or to be owned by foreign entities (M).

That is what it says. The money put into investment spending $(I_p + G + X)$ all gets saved as part of the total $(S + T + M)$.

All the elements of the Sectoral Balances equation represent money, either that which was put into spending as investment spending $(I_p + G + X)$ or where that money still exists and gets saved at the end of the given time period $(S + T + M)$.

The total amount of money, all of the money put into spending as investment, will be preserved somewhere. If more of that money ends up owned by foreign entities, or the government, less of it ends up in the private domestic economy.

That is what it means, that is all it means, that of the money used for spending, (X plus G plus I_p), all of it still exists somewhere.

Sectoral Balances

$(S - I_p)$ is a measure of how much S differs from private domestic investment I_p at the end of the given time period. If S is greater than I_p, then the total of exports minus imports plus the total of government spending minus taxes $[(G - T) + (X - M)]$ is greater than zero, meaning more money came into the private domestic sector than left it. If $[(G - T) + (X - M)]$ is less than zero, then that means more money left the private domestic economy than came into it. In that case S would be less than I_p.

What the Sectoral Balances equation, $S - I_p = (G - T) + (X - M)$, is not, is a measure of change in the level of wealth in each sector, other than that wealth called money. It is not a measure of production. And, in contrast to the modified expression for GDP, it is not a measure of ALL private domestic spending. For example, consumption (C), as I define it, is included in the expression for GDP but is not included in the Sectoral Balances equation. This is for the same reason the identity $S = I$ does not include C. The only spending it measures is spending that qualifies for being part of Keynes' I (my definition), which creates income in the private domestic sector, and spending that takes it out of the private domestic economy, causing that money to be owned by the foreign or government sectors.

The Sectoral Balances equation can be written in different ways if one wanted to examine it from different angles. Personally, I find the first of these three versions to give the most accurate portrayal of what the Sectoral Balances equation tells us:

$S = I_p + (G - T) + (X - M)$

$(S - I_p) = (G - T) + (X - M)$

$(S - I_p) + (T - G) + (M - X) = 0$

Sectoral Balances

~~~~~

We had to simplify it by making the proviso that all of T is paid for out of current income, and we also assume that all imports are paid for out of current income. If we do that, this gives us the Sectoral Balances equation.

Sometimes when I am putting my ideas in my model to paper (electrons?) I get new insights into ways to make the model simpler. Such is the case here, as it just occurred to me what might possibly be a better way to look at Taxes and Imports in the Sectoral Balances equation.

For taxes. Let us assume we make the rule that, before it could be used to pay taxes, all money MUST first have been put into spending, and created income in the private domestic economy. That includes money that, other than being used to pay taxes, was not intended to be used for any spending in the given time period. That money, must first be activated, i.e., considered as having been used for investment spending before being used to pay the taxes. We can recognize that this is actually the case if someone pays out of their bank account because the first step in the spending of that money is the person liquidates a portion of the value of their asset called a bank account by having the bank pay the depositor money to reduce the debt obligation the bank has to the depositor. This will count as investment spending, as defined in Chapter 2 of "Enlightened Capitalism", which would become part of private domestic income and then, when used to pay taxes, count as having taxes being paid for out of current income. See my previous comments on spending without money moving.

Let us assume that the entity was going to pay their taxes with physical money that was not in the bank but in their possession. In that case they could first "activate" the money by saying they paid it to themselves, creating income for themselves which would count as investment spending. That would mean if they were used as payment for taxes, those taxes could be considered as having been paid for by money acquired as current income. Allowing these two accounting strategies would guarantee that all Taxes are paid for out of current income.

We could do a similar reasoning for imports

That would mean we would *always* consider all taxes and all imports paid for out of current income, an assumption we had to make to derive the Sectoral Balances equation as it is normally taught. Using this way to look at money used to pay taxes and for imports then it could always be considered true that:

Savings = I_p + (G – T) + (X - M)

At any rate, we have assumed that all M and T in the Sectoral Balances equation is paid for out of current income so we can move forward in our analysis with even more certainty that this can be considered true.

The savings equals investment identity focuses on where the money that was put into investment ends up. That money does end up saved "in someone's pocket", at the end of the given time period. That is, the money still exists owned somewhere by someone at the end of that time period, unless it was destroyed or removed by the Central Bank.

The Sectoral Balances equation is really just a version of the savings equals investment identity, where S refers to what is left of the money put into spending that remains in the private domestic economy. The difference is that some of that money would have come from outside the private domestic economy so it could end up as part of S (G and X), and some money leaves the private domestic economy to become owned by the government or by foreigners (T and M) so it would be subtracted off the total for S. But the essence of the savings equals investment identity remains, and that is that all the money put into private domestic spending will be saved and still exist somewhere, owned by entities in the private domestic sector, the government sector, or the foreign sector.

The elements of the Sectoral Balances equation, X, M, G and T, are only measuring transactions involving those elements that are occurring between the private domestic sector and either the foreign sector or the government sector . There are no measurements of money exchanged directly between the foreign and government sectors.

For example, if a foreigner wants to purchase a Treasury Bond, in order for that transaction to be able to be accounted for in the Sectoral Balances equation, that foreigner would have to purchase the bond from a private domestic entity, such as a domestic Commercial Bank. That is, the private domestic Commercial Bank mediates the transaction.

This is typically what happens anyway. For example, the foreign sector entity purchases a bank deposit from the private domestic Commercial Bank, making the money used owned by the private domestic Commercial Bank. The foreign entity directs the spending of that money to buy a Treasury bond, the money becomes owned by the Treasury, the bond has been purchased and is given to the foreign entity. The bond is not money, it is an asset, a form of wealth. It is an asset whose value is based on a debt obligation of the Treasury to the bond holder. The Sectoral Balances equation only records that the foreign sector has less money and the private domestic sector has more money until such time as the Treasury bond is purchased at which point the private domestic sector no longer owns that money and the Treasury comes to own more money. The Sectoral Balances equation does not record the value of the bond or who owns it, nor does it record the debt obligation of the Treasury, since those are forms of wealth other than money, they get recorded on the wealth axis. Interest payments also need to be shown as involving Commercial Banks, with the money being paid first as domestic currency, until and unless it gets exchanged for foreign currency.

Before I start the next chapter I just want to make a few general comments on my understanding of *how proponents of the Sectoral Balances concept interpret the meaning of the elements making up the accounting of each sector*.

In the expression $(S - I_p)$ S is looked at as what is saved and therefore, when S increases, this is looked at as increasing the total amount of money saved or earned and/or the increase in wealth of the private domestic sector. And I_p is the amount of private domestic money spent and no longer possessed, and the wealth reduction in the private domestic sector caused by this spending.

[In reality this investment spending, I_p, is money put into spending in the private domestic economy which will become saved at the end of the given time period unless it went to the government or foreign sector. It does not represent loss of wealth, and does not even represent loss of money by the private sector. It is just added to the amount of money being used for spending and this will cause an increase in S (which money could possibly be further spent and lead to an increase in T and/or M).]

For the government sector, (T - G), T is taxes and the government income, increasing the amount of money and other wealth the government gets during that time period, and G is the amount of spending by the government which causes the money to go to the private domestic sector and the government wealth will be reduced by that amount. [Not generally recognized is that T must include any money paid from the private domestic sector to the government, not just taxes]

And for the foreign sector, (M − X) M represents the money earned, and wealth increase going to foreigners for selling their imports and X represents the money used by foreigners to buy exports and the reduction in wealth caused to foreigners by paying for exports.

CHAPTER 9
MMT Alleges that Increasing Government Debt is Required to have Increasing Private Domestic Wealth

MMT PROPONENTS IMPLY, and are pretty consistent in implying, that the Sectoral Balances equation shows us that government debt is not a bad thing, saying in fact, it is actually a necessary thing for us to have private domestic growth. The only caveat would be that, if the private domestic economy runs a trade surplus we may not need government debt or as much government debt to have the private domestic sector's economy grow. This is all derived from how they understand the Sectoral Balances equation and what it tells us.

MMT uses the following terminology. If the government sector's income minus spending (T - G), is greater than zero they say the government is running a "fiscal surplus", and if less than zero the government is running a "fiscal deficit". If T-G equals zero we have a balanced budget. If the foreign sector's income minus spending (M-X) is greater than zero that is said to represent a trade deficit

MMT Alleges that Increasing Government Debt

for the private domestic sector but a trade surplus for the foreign trading partners, and if M-X is less than zero it means the opposite, a trade surplus for the private domestic sector and a trade deficit for the foreign sector. If M-X equals zero we have balanced trade.

According to my model, for this to be fully accurate, the values T-G and M-X must be solely measurements of money, the spending of money and where that money ends up. Other than money, they cannot include any measurements of wealth. T-G and M-X cannot include the values of purely financial assets or their associated debt obligations, and they cannot include any measures describing the value of non-monetary real wealth. T-G and M-X are elements of the Sectoral Balances equation, which is a version of the Savings equals Investment equation. The Savings equals Investment identity shows how all the money being used for spending ends up saved. The Sectoral Balances equation then, to be a true identity, must show the same thing. The Sectoral Balances equation is a little more sophisticated in that it shows, in more detail, where the money used for spending comes from and where it may end up "saved", other than just the private domestic sector. In both cases they strictly measure all the money used for spending, in the given time period, and where it ends up. The modified expenditure approach to GDP is a version of Y = Keynes' I + Keynes' C and purely a measurement of spending and all spending involving the private domestic economy. The modified expenditure approach to GDP allows one to define what elements are part of Keynes' I which then allows the derivation of the Sectoral Balances equation. Thus, to be properly applied, all elements of the Sectoral Balances equation, $S-I_p$, T-G, and M-X, must be solely measures of money being used for spending and where that money ends up.

The terms fiscal deficit, fiscal surplus, trade deficit, and trade surplus are all in common use in economics today. And generally, people using those terms are including measures of spending and/or measures of wealth, possibly including non-monetary real wealth

MMT Alleges that Increasing Government Debt

and/or purely financial assets and the associated debt obligations, in what they are describing when they use one of those terms. Thus, I assume MMT advocates believe that it is proper that when they use these phrases they can also be referring to things measured in terms of both wealth (other than money) and spending. However, in the application we are discussing now, since MMT proponents are going to derive their conclusions from the Sectoral Balances equation, then, when they apply the terms fiscal deficit, fiscal surplus, trade deficit, and trade surplus they cannot have the determination as to when each of these terms should be used, be influenced by any measures of wealth other than money, where it comes from, and where it ends up. Once one decides to add measurements of wealth (other than money) to determining what the values the elements of the Sectoral Balances equation take, and when each of those terms should be applied, the Sectoral Balances equation will lose its "status" as an "identity, true at all times and in all situations". If an equation loses its status as an identity then conclusions drawn from the application of that equation are no longer reliably true. If MMT theorists want to use the Sectoral Balances equation as a basis for any conclusions, and if they want their conclusions to depend on the Sectoral Balances equation's status as a true identity, then, when those theorists use the terms fiscal deficit, fiscal surplus, trade deficit, and trade surplus they cannot include measurements of wealth, other than money, in determining when it is proper for any of those terms to be used.

It might provide a clearer picture if when one is using those terms during a discussion of the meaning of the Sectoral Balances equation (and is not including any measures of wealth other than money in the interpretation of the meaning of the elements of the Sectoral Balances equation), one uses the term "fiscal money surplus/deficit" instead of fiscal surplus/deficit. And uses the term "trade money surplus/deficit" instead of trade surplus/deficit.

The idea of using identities in economic models is that it could possibly allow the economist to include measures of massive amounts of various things and then, quoting the "identity" to say this shows that, at the end of the day, the total value of the measurements of that first massive group of various things is equal to the value of the measurements of the second massive group of various things. And they can do that without actually measuring the values of one or the other, or even both, of the groups. It gives the economist almost a magical tool for analyzing their economic models. But things cannot truly be identities unless they are clearly defined as to how and why, and are properly applied. If the identity is NOT a true identity (true at all times and in all situations), such as is the case with the "Fundamental Identity of National Income Accounting" then the application of such an "identity" can give false and misleading results.

I want to look at the Sectoral Balances equation to address this claim that we need to run a trade surplus X>M and/or a fiscal deficit G>T in order for the private domestic sector to run a surplus (S>I_p). The implication is that this means that for the private domestic economy to have increased wealth, other sectors need to have deficits.

If the foreign sector buys more exports than it gets paid for the imports it sells, more money is going to the private domestic economy, as a reward for producing the goods and services sold to the foreign sector. This will cause the private domestic sector to have more money. This is the result of a trade money surplus for the private domestic sector.

For the government sector to be contributing money to this private domestic sector "money surplus" this means they must give more money to the private domestic sector than they get back as income. This, the government can only do until they run out of money. At some point, if taxes cannot be increased, the government needs to borrow. This makes up for the difference between government spending and government income since now government borrowing will increase T to the amount of total spending by the government G. But this is a situation where the government is not

MMT Alleges that Increasing Government Debt

running a "fiscal money deficit" and the private domestic sector is not gaining more money than it loses. This does not describe a justification for the allegation that a government fiscal money deficit is causing increased private domestic money wealth.

How is it then that Sectoral Balances and MMT proponents reach that apparently false conclusion? That conclusion being that government borrowing causes the private domestic sector to be gaining more money and the government sector to be losing it.

The answer is they appear able to reach that conclusion for a couple reasons. The first one is that they do not include money loaned to the government as government income and part of T. The purchase of a bond from the Treasury, (for example), is spending, targeted at producing income for the government, to purchase a debt obligation from the Treasury. This is the transfer of ownership of money from the private domestic sector to the government and certainly counts as spending, and should be part of T. But, improperly, that amount of spending is not added to the value T takes. This means that a certain amount of money that should be accounted for in the Sectoral Balances equation is not, and that money is lost to our accounting, and will not, at the end of the given time period, be included as part of the money saved that is the preservation of investment spending. As a result, the Sectoral Balances equation loses its status as an identity. This shows up as an error where even though there is no fiscal money deficit, that even though with T properly defined, T-G should be shown as equaling zero, instead we have the value of T-G reported as less than zero. This allows MMT advocates to conclude there is such a money deficit.

The second thing that might be used to justify the belief that government deficit is causing the private domestic wealth to increase, is pointing to the measures of wealth caused by bond creation as the cause. Specifically, MMT advocates might be saying, (for example in the case of a Treasury Bond), that the Treasury agreeing to

MMT Alleges that Increasing Government Debt

a debt obligation and the private domestic sector receiving an asset called a Treasury Bond is wealth "flowing" from the Treasury to the private domestic sector. Of course, they would be ignoring the "flow" of money from the private domestic sector to the Treasury (the spending to purchase the bond), but they would include the "flow" of wealth from the Treasury to the private domestic sector as if it were money leaving the Treasury and going to the private domestic sector. This would be a way to justify saying that the government sector is running a fiscal deficit caused by the creation and sale of Treasury bonds. Which would allow them to infer that government borrowing is equivalent to the private domestic sector gaining money and the government losing money.

It is quite likely that MMT advocates would not acknowledge that is what is occurring, but my model allows me to allege that this is exactly what is happening. The reality is, however, I don't think one can understand my argument, unless one also understands that the "Fundamental Identity of National Income Accounting" is not an identity and how spending of money, and measures of wealth need to be calculated on different axes.

It's perfectly ok to say that since one sector has gained assets and the other sector has gained debt obligations, that, limited to those two things, the one with assets has more wealth and the one with more debt obligations has less wealth. But if you want to look at the whole picture, you must include the fact that the lender paid money to the borrower to gain possession of those assets. Coming to the conclusion that, almost by definition, government debt causes private domestic sector wealth, is caused by a misinterpretation of what the Sectoral Balances equation can tell us.

Contrary to this interpretation of Sectoral Balances given by MMT advocates, that government borrowing directly causes increased private domestic wealth, creating a purely financial asset does not cause any change in the total level of wealth in either sector.

MMT Alleges that Increasing Government Debt

When a purely financial asset is created, spending is required to cause it to exist. Spending is also required for the ownership of a purely financial asset to go from one sector to another. This is what happens when a Treasury bond is issued and sold. The private domestic sector pays to purchase the bond, and money goes from the private domestic sector to the Treasury. The asset, the bond, is created, and the private domestic sector then owns the bond, but has lost the money it spent for the bond causing the total wealth of the private domestic sector to be unchanged. Meanwhile, the Treasury has lost wealth by agreeing to a debt obligation, but has gained the money paid to acquire the bond, and this means, the total wealth of the government remains unchanged. The transaction where a private domestic sector is purchasing a debt obligation from the government causes no change in the level of wealth for either sector.

The money, where it comes from and where it goes are the only things measured by the Sectoral Balances equation. Neither the asset called a bond, nor the Treasury's debt obligation, contribute to the values the elements of the Sectoral Balances equation take. The asset and debt obligation are not descriptions of spending and are things that must be accounted for on the wealth axis.

A Treasury debt arising when a purely financial asset is created is not the same thing as an amount of spending causing income to be created. The agreeing to a debt obligation causing wealth to "flow" from the Treasury to the private domestic sector is not interchangeable with the spending done, and the income created, when a debt obligation is being purchased. Spending is money moving around changing ownership, and each time that happens to a given amount of money, new income is created. But debt obligations and purely financial assets are formed simultaneously and the value of each is forever linked, or at least until the debt is fully paid or written off. Spending is accounted for on the spending/money income axis and the values of debt obligations and purely financial assets are accounted for on the wealth axis.

MMT Alleges that Increasing Government Debt

As I mentioned, the only thing elements of Sectoral Balances measure is money, money spending and where it ends up. If T properly includes all payments to the government sector including taxes and money loaned to the government by the private domestic sector, what ends up showing in the elements of Sectoral Balances equation from the purchase of a Treasury bond is T increasing, and S decreasing as money moves from the private domestic sector to the Treasury.

But if payments for the Treasury bond are not shown as part of T then the value of S will not change and neither will the value of T. The payment for the bonds is not recorded. And if one pretends that the creation of the treasury debt and the formation of the asset called a Treasury bond, can be described as wealth "flowing" from the Treasury to the private domestic sector, and that is equivalent to the spending of that amount of money, then one would probably want to add the value of that presumed "spending" to the Sectoral Balances equation. But in that case, since wealth was flowing from the Treasury to the private domestic sector, T would have to show as decreased, and S would have to show as increased. This would mean that the only thing the records show is the Treasury getting debt and private domestic sector getting a bond with no evidence of anyone paying for the bond. This could be interpreted as saying that Treasury borrowing is equivalent to the Treasury getting more debt and the private domestic sector getting a Treasury bond for free.

Let us look at another angle that may help us understand how **ignoring** the fact that all money paid by the private domestic sector to the government must be part of T, will invalidate the Sectoral Balances equation's status as an identity. Let us say the income and spending for all three sectors was balanced. This would mean $S - I_p$ equals zero, M - X equals zero, and T - G equals zero. But for MMT, T represents only taxes paid and does not include money paid for bonds. Since all sectors are balanced, the Treasury spending, G, must equal T, that is, G is equivalent to the amount of taxes paid during the time period in question. But that would mean that the government sector is running a surplus because the government is collecting ownership of all that money paid for both the Treasury bonds and the amount collected as taxes. Yet if T – G equals zero, the Treasury could only have spent an amount of money equal to the taxes collected. If the Treasury did not spend the money it was paid as compensation for the bonds it issued, as it could not if T represents only taxes paid and, at the same time, equals G, then that money paid for bonds would be collecting in the government coffers as a surplus. But it is stated in this scenario that the government budget is balanced, so that money cannot be collecting, it must have never been spent, and that means it must have stayed in the private domestic sector as part of S. In addition, the private domestic sector has come to own the Treasury bond as well and, in that way, has an increase in wealth. This leads to the same conclusion, that not including all money paid from the private domestic sector to the government as part of T will be the same as saying the government is giving Treasury bonds to the private domestic sector for free. That is what this wrong interpretation of Sectoral Balances will show on paper, and that is not what is happening at all.

As for the Treasury paying off debt, normally one would consider this as included in the element G, and this should show up in the equation for Sectoral Balances as the transfer of ownership of money from the Treasury to the private domestic sector represented by an increase in S. But this scenario of adding measures of wealth to the Sectoral Balances calculations, as if interchangeable with spending, has given us the result that buying a Treasury bond is equivalent to the Treasury transferring money from the Treasury to the private domestic sector. To be consistent this should also mean that paying off a Treasury bond is the flow of wealth from the private domestic sector to the treasury and is **equivalent to** a transfer of **money** from the private domestic sector to the Treasury causing an increase in T and decrease in S!

∽∞∞∽

Having spent so much time talking about the wrong way to interpret the meaning of the elements of the Sectoral Balances equation, I would like to make some comments on the proper way to understand this equation and its elements.

Sectoral Balances tells us nothing about wealth other than the form of wealth known as (base) money. Each element in the Sectoral Balances equation is a measure of base money and the spending of same.

The modified expression for GDP I have derived is a measurement of spending and income occurring involving entities in the private domestic economy. I have alleged and still do, that the modified expression for the expenditure approach to GDP I presented earlier, must be the correct expression, if this expression is going to be purely an accounting of spending and income and include ALL the spending and income involving the private domestic economy. You will note that since the modified expression for GDP is an accounting of private domestic spending and income, it does not include spending occurring directly between the government and the foreign sector. Despite that, Sectoral Balances proponents treat it as if the different sectors can be considered totally balanced and symmetrical where each sector is equivalent in how they interact with the other sectors. Since, in my model, the Sectoral Balances equation is derived from the modified expenditure approach to GDP, and since the modified expenditure approach to GDP does not include spending occurring directly between the Government and the foreign sector, then such spending will not be included in the values the elements of the Sectoral Balances equation take.

MMT Alleges that Increasing Government Debt

It is possible to develop a model where the accounting of spending occurring directly between the foreign sector and the domestic government is included. I am just saying that the Sectoral Balances equation derived from the modified expression for the expenditure approach equation is not such a model. If the Sectoral Balances equation is going to be a true identity, then it cannot include any spending occurring directly between the government and the foreign sector. Discussions relevant to this issue are included in Chapters 31, 40, 42, and Chapters 49 to 51 of "Enlightened Capitalism: A Keynes Primer, 2nd Edition".

I would like to review what the individual elements of the Sectoral Balances equation, properly understood, measure:

S is the amount of money that has been used for spending and caused income in the private domestic sector, which ends up owned by private domestic sector entities at the end of the given time period.

I_p is the amount of money put into spending for the first time in the given time period by private domestic entities creating income for other entities in the private domestic economy.

G is the amount of money spent by the government aimed at creating income in the private domestic economy. It is a measure of how much money has left the government and become owned by the private domestic sector.

T is the amount of spending done by entities in the private domestic sector that has created income for the government. This includes taxes but also includes paying money to the government for bonds, which is the private domestic sector lending to the government, and in fact any payment from the private domestic sector to the government including any other payment for goods and services that would not be considered taxes or lending. T specifically measures the amount of money that has left the private domestic sector and become owned by the government.

MMT Alleges that Increasing Government Debt

X is the amount of money put into spending and creating income in the private domestic sector as payment for exports. It is the amount of money that has had its ownership transferred from the foreign sector to entities in the private domestic sector. First, normally, the foreigner may need to exchange their currency for domestic currency before this payment can occur.

M is the amount of spending by private domestic entities to pay for imports and is a measure of how much money leaves the private domestic sector and becomes owned by foreigners.

If the private domestic sector gives more money to the government and foreigners, then the private domestic sector owns less money. This would be occurring for any payments made to the government including paying for Treasury bonds. That is the only thing recorded in the Sectoral Balances equation that says anything about the effect of Treasury borrowing on private domestic wealth. More lending to the Treasury causes the Treasury to have more money and the private domestic sector to have less money. More lending, that is, spending by private domestic sector entities to purchase Treasury bonds, causes an increase in T and a decrease in the amount left to be saved in the private domestic sector, that is, it causes S to be decreased.

The wealth known as a Treasury bond, which is an asset, and the measure of "negative" wealth known as a debt obligation are not recorded anywhere in the Sectoral Balances equation. They are measures of wealth and recorded on the wealth axis. If the terms fiscal deficit/surplus are used to describe measures of wealth other than money, there cannot be any conclusions about debt or fiscal deficits or fiscal surpluses derived from the Sectoral Balances equation, since, if the Sectoral Balances equation is defined in such a way that it represents a true identity, it does not measure wealth or changes in the level of wealth, except that wealth known as (base) money.

Even though we know that spending is often associated with the creation of wealth, there is no entry in the Sectoral Balances equation

MMT ALLEGES THAT INCREASING GOVERNMENT DEBT

that records how much wealth may be created by the movements of ownership of money recorded in the elements of Sectoral Balances. There is nothing in the Sectoral Balances concept that says debt in one sector, a measure of wealth, creates wealth in another sector. There is no accounting of how much wealth is created or the type of wealth created. If there is balanced trade, there is nothing in the Sectoral Balances equation that supports the idea that increased wealth cannot occur in the private sector unless debt is occurring in the government sector. Why? Because other than the money used for spending, the Sectoral Balances equation does not measure wealth, only the spending of that money, where it comes from and where it ends up.

Since spending and wealth are different things that need to be measured on their own axes, we know that the wealth creation occurring during a given period where a given amount of money spending has occurred can take many different forms and be appraised as having many different possible monetary values. We also know that the same amount of wealth creation can be associated with many different levels of money spending.

It is very possible to have wealth created when the government is running a deficit, where total debt obligations are increasing, but it also very possible to have wealth creation when the government is paying down its debt. In either case T, properly defined, will match G and there will be no government "fiscal money deficit" because any money received by the government would be immediately spent to pay off debt or for any other expenses.

In fact, if you think about it, theoretically, the private sector could function as a fully autonomous economy. Spending could occur, incomes be created, and this spending could stimulate wealth production solely with activity that occurs in the private domestic economy and with no interaction with the government or foreign sector at all. I only say "theoretically" because the government serves an important role in providing stability in a country, but you get the point. It is not

MMT Alleges that Increasing Government Debt

necessary for the government to run a deficit, and continually increase debt, in order for the private domestic economy to grow.

All the Sectoral Balances equation is, is an equation showing that all money put in to spending in the given time period will still exist somewhere at the end of the given time period. That is the essence of the "Savings equals Investment" identity. The Sectoral Balances equation, properly defined, is basically a form of the Savings equals Investment equation. It remains an identity if you count as savings all the money that has, in the current time period, been used for spending and created income in the private domestic economy, including money that, later spending of caused it to leave the private domestic economy and become owned by the government or foreigners.

It seems to me that the interpretation that government deficits cause creation of private domestic wealth, (if you believe that money spending and wealth creation are equivalent), is implying that somehow steadily increasing government debt, by selling bonds, is equivalent to creating more money. But, theoretically, government debt can be created and increased to any level with the same size (base) money supply. For example, the fact is the same amount of base money could be used over and over and over again to keep purchasing new Treasury bonds. The money is given to the Treasury for the bonds, the money is spent by the government and becomes income for private domestic sector entities who can then use the same money to buy more bonds, causing more money to become owned by the Treasury who again uses it for spending causing the money to go back to being owned in the private domestic sector, which money can then be used to buy more Treasury bonds etc., etc. As long as the Treasury wants to keep issuing and selling bonds, and as long as enough other entities want to keep purchasing these bonds, the same (base) money supply can be used for the spending needed to purchase those bonds.

MMT Alleges that Increasing Government Debt

All the measurements of the debt obligations and the purely financial assets known as Treasury bonds are measured on the wealth axis. The spending to purchase them is what should be shown on the Sectoral Balances equation, and it is the spending to purchase them that gives the government part of the money it needs for government spending (G).

If all these debt obligations and Treasury bonds created were treated like it was money, it would make it look like Treasury bond creation is causing the money supply to grow, which would also, presumably, be interpreted by Sectoral Balances advocates as a greater and greater amount of wealth in the economy.

Creating purely financial assets like Treasury bonds does not create a change in wealth level unless the money used to buy the purely financial asset was used again for further spending which led to the creation of non-financial real assets.

It is very clear that MMT proponents interpret Sectoral Balances as stating that, if we have balanced trade, it is not possible to have private domestic sector growth without government debt, and that in every time period, if we want private domestic sector growth, we have to continue to increase government debt. Therefore, according to them, if we have balanced trade, and run a balanced budget, it will prevent any economic growth in the private domestic sector. And if they say that about a balanced budget then by extension, they would say having a government surplus, such as we would have if we were reducing and paying down our national debt, would cause the private domestic economy to shrink.

Even the focus on exports and imports is meaningless in terms of talking about their effect on private domestic wealth. If foreigners are buying exports from the private domestic sector, the Sectoral

MMT Alleges that Increasing Government Debt

Balances equation says they are money losers and the private domestic entities who sold the exports are money gainers, and therefore the government may not need to have a fiscal money deficit, or as big of a fiscal money deficit, in order for the private domestic sector to have more money. But nothing is able to be determined about what happens to wealth. The Sectoral Balances equation just records where the money goes, when properly defined that is, not what is happening to wealth overall.

I believe that what is attractive to MMT theorists, about the significance of their interpretation of what conclusions may be drawn from the Sectoral Balances equation, is that it allows them to desensitize people to the possible adverse effects of debt. I mean what could be a better way to alleviate people's anxiety and have them support more borrowing than to say, not only is it not harmful, but that it is beneficial. But then they take it further, to the point where they allege they have proven it is REQUIRED to increase government debt, or at least have a combination of government fiscal deficit and a trade surplus, in order for there to be any private domestic economic growth. **I would allege that all three "sectors" can have growth in wealth at the same time.**

When we properly understand the Sectoral Balances equation as just a measure of money spending and where it ends up at the end of the given time period, it is not clear to me what benefit we derive from it. On the other hand, when it is not properly understood or applied it can lead to a lot of damaging interpretations and recommendations.

The ultimate policy recommendations MMT gives does not require any contribution from the Sectoral Balances concept. The ultimate policy recommendations MMT gives does not require

MMT Alleges that Increasing Government Debt

us to believe government debt is required to have private domestic wealth. But my belief is the Sectoral Balances concept and the wrong interpretation of what it means, is used by MMT proponents to support the idea of, and desensitize people from worries about, the dangers of excessive government borrowing. By treating government debt obligations as if they were money, the supply of which continues to increase, and by making it seem that we need to have this debt continue to increase to have a functioning economy, then the idea would be, that if we desensitize people about creating debt as a worry, we can also desensitize people about possible negative effects of creating too much money.

I have stayed away from talking about Central Bank spending in these discussions of Sectoral Balances. This is because we do not lose much by doing so and it allows my model to be presented in a less complicated form. If included, Central Bank spending, to purchase the purely financial assets it is allowed to purchase, counts as money put into spending for the first time in the given time period and is part of G. It would then increase the value of S, the amount of money used for spending and considered saved at the end of the given time period. This being true unless that same money becomes used to pay for T or M.

When the Central Bank sells assets this would theoretically be part of T, payments from the private domestic sector to the government (Central Bank). But since this causes the money to be owned by the Central Bank it has left the money supply and reduced it by that amount. The end result of that, is there is no effect on totals for T, but the amount of money left over to be considered saved at the end of the given time period is reduced by that amount (S is reduced). But this is why I do not include payments to the Central Bank as part of what needs to be included in T.

MMT Alleges that Increasing Government Debt

The main policy recommendations coming from MMT come from the theories of Abba Lerner known as "functional finance". Functional finance has its own drawbacks, separate from the problems caused by misinterpretations of the meaning of the Sectoral Balances equation, and will be discussed later.

I would also mention that borrowing may be necessary and desirable to pay for some government spending, which spending may have the effect of leading to increased production of wealth. But I would further add that this spending could alternatively be paid for by taxing. MMT might criticize this statement, saying taxing has the same effect on the economy as reducing government spending. This would be showing the influence of functional finance on their thinking. But the reality is, that money obtained from taxes can then be used for more spending and may lead to an increase in government spending (G). This would be especially true if the taxes were designed to be a progressive tax, where those who have higher incomes pay a larger percentage of their income in taxes. This could cause an overall increase in private domestic income, and lead to increased wealth production as well. I am saying that taxing does not have to be associated with decreased income in the private domestic sector or decreased wealth production. Properly implemented, the opposite could be true. That further negates the idea that government debt is required to have a growing private domestic economy.

CHAPTER 10

THE FUNCTION OF TREASURY BORROWING

DESPITE WHAT MMT says, the function of Treasury borrowing is to get funds to pay for Treasury spending. *That* is the function of borrowing, it is not any of these other functions alleged by MMT theorists:

1. It is not done so we can run a deficit "because you need to run a deficit to have a private domestic surplus". Because you don't need to.

2. It would not be done to decrease private domestic reserves so as to increase interest rates. This is so because the Treasury would not be borrowing if it had enough money and therefore one can assume that the money will be spent quickly and go right back into private domestic reserves. As a result, the effect on interest rates is fleeting at best. The concept discussed here in '2' applies to the Open Market Operations era, prior to IOER.

3. The Treasury issuing bonds, sold on the primary market, does not directly affect the total base money supply, since with the initial purchase of the bonds, normally done by

private domestic entities, the money goes from the private domestic entities where it is in the money supply to the Treasury where it remains in the money supply, assuming we are using my definition of the base money supply.

4. A Treasury does not issue bonds to make up for the fact that the value of bonds possessed on the Central Bank's balance sheet is zero, which would cause there to be no assets to sell in order to reduce the money supply. First off, the assets the Central Bank buys to increase the money supply and add to their balance sheet are plentiful. They already exist and are generally owned by private entities. The total value of these assets is in the neighborhood of 18 trillion dollars in the United States at the current time.[3] So, there is no need to create more Treasury Bonds to give the Central Bank the ability to increase the money supply and its balance sheet in the usual way.

But even if there were zero safe government backed purely financial assets on the Central Bank's balance sheet, that can be sold to reduce the money supply, the solution would not be to have the Treasury issue more bonds This solution is no solution because it is basically saying that first we must increase the money supply by having the Central Bank buy more Treasury bonds, so the Central Bank has Treasury bonds to sell to decrease the money supply. Or to put it more simply, that is the same thing as saying the Central Bank has to increase the money supply so it can then decrease the money supply by the same amount. (Which is ridiculous!).

Should the amount of sellable assets on the Central Bank's balance sheet reach zero, the only way to decrease the money supply would be to destroy money with nothing earned in return for it, other than facilitating economic stability. Call it an economic stability tax or something. The Treasury can be the one to destroy it,

---

3   https://fred.stlouisfed.org/series/FDHBPIN

The Function of Treasury Borrowing

earning nothing in return or the money could just be transferred to ownership of the Central Bank, without the Central Bank giving anything in return. As soon as the Central Bank owns it, it is out of the money supply and in essence no longer exists.

CHAPTER 11
Interest Rates on Bonds And IOER

Does Borrowing by the Treasury Cause Interest Rates on Bonds to Increase?

AS FOR FUNDS available to buy Treasury bonds, because all the base money borrowed by the Treasury gets immediately spent, all that money returns to the private sector, most of it going back into Commercial Bank reserves. This means it will remain available for the purpose of buying more Treasury bonds. This would be true unless all the remaining money is tied up somewhere, where it cannot be used for that purpose. An example would be where money owned by the Commercial Banks was needed to meet the mandate to keep cash around as part of required reserves. If no or little cash was available to meet Treasury borrowing needs, the interest rates on the bonds may need to be increased, to attract more buyers.

Today, however, Commercial Banks have large quantities of excess reserves. So large that they have the ability to keep buying and buying Treasury bonds with almost no limit in sight until the Treasury decides not to borrow any more, or until interest rates were driven down to the point where the incentive to buy bonds disappears. This would occur when the interest rate earned from buying Treasury bonds was reduced to the point where it was no longer the most profitable option.

IOER

One of the main reasons banks have such large amounts of reserves is due to a change in how the economy is managed by the Central Bank.

I am specifically referring to the practice of the Central Bank of the United States, instituted in 2008 based on laws passed by Congress in 2006, of paying interest to Commercial Bank on their reserves (cash owned by Commercial Banks). This would not be such an issue if they only paid interest on required reserves since banks had to keep that amount of money anyway. But it is the paying interest on excess reserves that really causes distortions in the market, giving banks less incentive to lend.

In the era we now have, instead of Open Market Operations determining the federal funds rate, we have the interest rate the Central Bank is paying Commercial Banks on their excess reserves (IOER rate) determining the federal funds rate. In this situation, when the Treasury wants to borrow, it would have to offer interest rates no lower than IOER rate. Otherwise, the Commercial Banks could keep the money as excess reserves and collect that IOER interest.

Even though the Central Bank pays the interest on excess reserves, it is ultimately the Treasury, i.e., the taxpayer who pays for that IOER interest. This is because IOER is paid for out of the Central Bank's operating costs. The Central Bank's operating expenses are paid for out of interest the Central Bank earns, in large

Interest Rates on Bonds and IOER

part collected from the Treasury when it pays interest on Treasury Bonds on the Central Bank's balance sheet. After the Central Bank pays for its operating expenses, any of the money the Central Bank received as interest "earnings" that remains unspent, is given to the Treasury.

What this means is that since IOER payments to Commercial Banks are considered operating expenses for the Central Bank, paying IOER will reduce the amount of money "refunded" to the Treasury. This, in essence, means the Treasury is paying for the IOER.

I have seen where MMT refers to IOER as a HOLDING RATE. And, in my opinion, they fail to describe IOER for what it is, the taxpayers giving Commercial Banks money for doing nothing. Is it possible that MMT proponents think this is equivalent to Open Market Operations? Or perhaps they think it is even better because the Central Bank does not need to be doing all that sometimes complicated and uncertain Open Market Operations? Do they not express concern about IOER because they don't think the Treasury and the Central Bank should be considered separate institutions? Or is it just that they think we worry too much about the government creating and spending more money in general?

CHAPTER 12
Functional Finance

KEYNES KNEW THAT, if unemployment was high, it was likely that if any extra spending was introduced into that economy this would, by having that same money used for further spending, cause an increase in total income that would be greater than the initial extra spending. He also knew that the more this money was likely to be used for spending again, the greater the effect on increasing total income, which he called the multiplier effect.

Keynes came up with the term "the propensity to consume" to be the fraction of current income people or entities will use for further spending. He reasoned that poor people are likely to spend a greater fraction of their income, so giving more income to poor people is likely to cause a greater effect on increasing total income and stimulating the economy than giving more income to rich people. The greater the likelihood of re-spending of the money, the greater the "propensity to consume" of that money, the larger will be the multiplier effect. Giving money to poor people, therefore, could be expected to cause a larger multiplier effect than giving it to rich people, because of poor people's higher likelihood of spending what they acquire as income. In "Enlightened Capitalism: A Keynes Primer" Chapters

33 to 36, I give what I think is a more accurate description of how the multiplier effect occurs.

Abba Lerner was an economist who studied with Keynes. He was very attuned to the idea of the multiplier effect. He believed, as Keynes did, that this concept opened the door to possible ways to mediate and prevent large swings in the state of the economy. His solution, as was Keynes', is that during times of depression and low unemployment, the government should spend more. Lerner also reasoned that during times when the economy appears to be overly stimulated, the government should reduce spending or increase taxes to reduce people's ability to spend. The indicator for whether the economy was overheated, i.e., too stimulated, was the level of inflation. If inflation was too high, we needed to tax or reduce spending. If, on the other hand, unemployment was a problem the solution would be to spend or reduce taxes.

These ideas are currently mainstream, and are part of the framework of ideas economists utilize when deciding on policy recommendations. These interventions are generally called "fiscal policy" as compared to "monetary policy", and both are discussed in "Enlightened Capitalism".

Lerner, however, believed that other economists and policy makers were not aggressive enough in implementation of policies intended to fight economic depressions.

Ultimately, he believed one should base their spending and taxing decisions on outcomes, not on the size of the money supply or the size of government debt. The two indicators he felt were the most important to monitor were the unemployment level and the inflation rate. Ideally, according to Lerner, policy makers should increase government spending up to the point where involuntary unemployment was non-existent, while keeping the inflation rate low. Since having zero involuntary unemployment with a low

Functional Finance

inflation rate is basically impossible, I imagine he would just say the policymakers should do the best they could.

Abba Lerner used the term "Functional Finance" for his model. He had three rules for applying his economic stimulus plan which I will paraphrase:

1. Use fiscal policy to manage unemployment and inflation levels. This may include increased Treasury spending or decreased taxing to decrease unemployment levels. And decreased Treasury spending and increased taxing to reduce inflation.

When unemployment was high, funding for the increased spending could include Treasury borrowing, or as some modern MMT proponents suggest, direct Central Bank funding of Treasury's spending.

During times of high inflation and low unemployment, if he decided to use taxation, it would not be done for the purpose of the Treasury gathering more funds for future Treasury spending. Instead, it would be for the purpose of slowing the economy to reduce inflation. MMT really favors the idea of the government just "printing" or borrowing what money it needs for government spending rather than having to depend on taxation to acquire it.

2. Use monetary policy by the Central Bank to keep interest rates at the level that maximizes employment, and keeps inflation manageable. This is something all economists would agree on.

3. If the first two steps are not effective enough, double down and be as aggressive as you need to be to meet the stated goals. If you must borrow to get enough funding, don't worry about the debt level, just worry about unemployment and inflation levels. Keep borrowing all you need, no matter how high the debt level gets. Borrow to make payments on debt and borrow more to

support Treasury spending. Presumably MMT advocates would prefer direct Central Bank funding of Treasury spending, if they could get it to happen.

I consider this approach to funding government spending to be dangerous. This is because it reduces and could eliminate the connection between human effort and those things government spending pays for. Taxing, to me, is a way to make sure we all help pay for government spending, and it demands we all act in a responsible fashion and contribute in some way to maintaining and improving our standard of living and quality of life. It requires most of us, at some point in our life, to work, put in the effort to do our jobs well and, to the degree we are able, earn income. Using taxing to pay for government spending means the politicians, who will direct the spending, need to act responsibly because they must be accountable to the taxpayers.

Borrowing with no limit to allowable levels of debt can weaken the connection between borrowing and the effort required to pay off the debt. It can reduce the motivation to work and contribute to paying off the debt while at the same time, help pay for all those things government spending provides. If debt is not of much concern, because the government can always borrow enough to pay the debt no matter how large it becomes, then we lose any sense of the value of money. We must keep track of and be concerned about the level of debt and the amount of borrowing and struggle to keep it manageable, and continue the effort to produce those things that allow us to maintain our standard of living. A rational guideline commonly espoused for what our limit on borrowing should be is that borrowing, in any given year, should not exceed GDP growth for that year, on the average.

I think it is an unrealistic fantasy to believe that we can prevent serious consequences just by focusing on the level of employment and the inflation rate, with no limits put on borrowing, or even worse by allowing direct Central Bank funding of Treasury spending (See my comments on colonial Virginia's currency in chapter 3).

If you think about it, both those things are really ways to avoid the taxation issue, both to avoid the need for politicians to spend tax revenue responsibly and for us to avoid the issue of having people pay taxes, especially the need to have those who have the most, pay the most.

At any rate, whenever you are reading about or trying to understand MMT, be aware that, at least by my understanding, MMT proponents' ultimate goal is to set up a system where functional finance is implemented.

"Knowledge of any kind belongs to those living beings who have studied, understood and mastered that material"

The author may be contacted at:

danbrightec@gmail.com

for any questions, comments or discussion

www.ingramcontent.com/pod-product-compliance
Lightning Source LLC
Chambersburg PA
CBHW031428210526
45464CB00005B/2099